THE
PRACTICALLY
VEGETARIAN
COOKBOOK

THE
PRACTICALLY
VEGETARIAN
COOKBOOK

JOSCELINE DIMBLEBY

Photography by Simon Wheeler

RANDOM HOUSE
NEW YORK

Random House, Inc., 201 East 50th Street, New York, NY 10022, USA.

© 1994 Websters International Publishers
Text copyright © 1994 Josceline Dimbleby
Photographs copyright © 1994 Websters International Publishers

Originally published in the United Kingdom
by Websters International Publishers Limited, London, in 1994.

Colour separation by Columbia Offset, Singapore
Printed and bound by Dai Nippon Printing, Hong Kong

Conceived, edited and designed by Websters International Publishers Limited,
Axe & Bottle Court, 70 Newcomen Street, London SE1 1YT, England.

Library of Congress Catalog Card Number 94-66994

ISBN 0-679-42585-3

98765432

First U. S. Edition

NOTES ON RECIPES

All spoon measures are level unless otherwise stated.
Eggs are standard size unless otherwise stated.
Pepper is freshly ground black pepper unless otherwise stated.
Milk is full-fat fresh milk unless otherwise stated.
Ovens should be preheated to the specified temperature.

▶ Opposite page, left to right:
*Peppers filled with garlic potatoes and cooked in olive oil (107); Vietnamese chicken
noodle hot pot with fresh leaves (95); carrot tart with candied carrot topping (139)*

CONTENTS

INTRODUCTION

I don't think I shall ever become a total vegetarian. My love of all food, of the wonderful variety now available, and of my freedom to try anything, would stop me. However, I have noticed that these days I eat far less meat and, indeed, don't miss it at all even when I haven't touched it for weeks. Vegetarianism has increased enormously over recent years but so, perhaps even more, has the number of people who have reduced their consumption of red meat to almost nothing, and concentrate instead on eating far more vegetables, as well as poultry and fish dishes which are combined with a large proportion of vegetables, or with grains such as rice or bulgur, with pasta or with legumes. In this way, they easily consume less animal fat and feel healthier and more energetic: in fact, the 'practically vegetarian' diet could be considered to provide the best of both worlds.

My philosophy of eating is a very straightforward – even old-fashioned – one. I am a firm believer that any normally healthy person is wisest to eat the most varied diet they can, remembering only the simple rule that they can eat what they want, but never too much of any one thing. There are so many different diets suggested nowadays that people with no specific medical reason to restrict themselves are sometimes persuaded to try a complicated way of eating – to cut out this or that ingredient or type of food often on the slightest of pretexts. This sort of thing induces worry, and worry is not healthy. We have to eat to live and luckily good food is one of the great joys of life; it promotes a feeling of happiness and well-being – and happiness is most definitely healthy.

I do love vegetables, with their magnificent variety of appetizing colors, textures and flavors, and this book has therefore been a great pleasure to work on. I have one vegetarian daughter and several vegetarian friends, and this gave me particular inspiration when dreaming up the strictly vegetable main dishes. The increasing availability of different kinds of vegetables offers endless scope for interesting combinations, and

◀ *Cod with sorrel and spinach purée in puff pastry packets (p83)*

vegetables can truly be a feast for the eye as well as the stomach. Gone are the days when all vegetarian dishes seemed to be varying shades of brown. Don't forget, too, that many of the vegetable main dishes can become 'practically vegetarian' by the judicious addition of slivers of poultry or fish.

Salads in particular have become much more interesting recently. We now have at our disposal not only some truly wonderful salad leaves but also nut oils and fruit and herb vinegars to combine with spices and seasonings in exciting dressings.

A large variety of legumes, grains and rice as well as both eggs and cheese greatly extend the culinary possibilities for any vegetarian. They also help to replace the proteins that would otherwise be provided by meat-based dishes and are useful for informal meals of any kind. Pasta has become a vital part of almost everyone's life; what would we do, arriving home late and tired to an almost empty refrigerator, if we did not have that packet of tagliatelle on the shelf and a bottle of extra virgin olive oil?

When it is really fresh and carefully cooked, fish is probably always my first choice. I still think of it as the 'brain food' I was told as a child it was, and it never makes you feel weighed down or bloated. The flavors are delicate, and textures light and succulent, and these days again there is a wider range of fish and shellfish available than ever before.

All kinds of poultry are a boon to the family cook. Inexpensive, versatile and loved by children, it is a great stand-by. Poultry adapts to almost any added ingredients or flavorings, and as you will see from my recipes, poultry dishes can be transformed into mild, homey dishes or something exotic, to suit your mood.

I could not produce any comprehensive collection of recipes without desserts. Desserts are my passion: fruit desserts, chocolate desserts, ice creams, gooey cakes – all kinds of desserts. I know that desserts cannot be said to be strictly necessary for a healthy diet, but they are fun to make and a pleasure to eat. The occasional indulgence is not going to do you any harm and will do a great deal to lift your spirits.

STARTERS & SOUPS

The start of a meal is crucial. It sets the tone, and is almost always the most remembered dish. Appetites are keen and your guests at their most observant and appreciative of the food, not yet distracted by conversation, and, possibly, by a fair amount of good wine. First courses can be inspiring in the same way as desserts because there is a chance for a bit of fantasy and artistry. And like desserts, since they are not an absolutely essential part of a meal, they seem more of a treat. If you are a true vegetarian, you could combine starters and vegetable side dishes to make a complete one-course main meal. Alternatively, just two of them could be used for a light meal served simply with some good bread – possibly one of the savory breads in the breads chapter. A first course must never be too filling; it is, after all, supposed to titillate the appetite for further good things. You should always choose something which has not only quite different ingredients to the main course, but contrasting color and texture too. Soups are always popular for summer or winter first courses, and look particularly special presented in a handsome tureen.

FRESH PLUM TOMATO AND BASIL TART WITH OLIVE OIL AND GARLIC CRUST

The crust of this summer tart can be baked 'blind' – baked before it has been filled – without needing to be weighted down in the usual way, and is still wonderfully crisp when filled. Try to use deep red plum tomatoes because their flavor is best for cooking.

FOR THE CRUST:
1½ cups all-purpose flour
1 teaspoon salt
2 large garlic cloves, finely chopped
5 tablespoons extra virgin olive oil
1 tablespoon water
FOR THE FILLING:
2 pounds plum tomatoes
2 tablespoons extra virgin olive oil
3–4 large garlic cloves, thinly sliced
2 teaspoons superfine sugar
¼ stick butter
12 fresh basil leaves, thinly sliced
6–8 fresh sage leaves (optional)
Salt and black pepper
Fresh basil and sage leaves, to
*   garnish (optional)*

◄ *Fresh plum tomato and basil tart with olive oil and garlic crust*

To make the crust, sift the flour and salt into a bowl. Put the garlic into a saucepan with the olive oil and place the pan over a medium heat for about two minutes. Remove the pan from the heat and stir in the water. Pour this hot mixture gradually into the flour, stirring it with a wooden spoon to form a dough. Then, using your fingers, press pieces of the crumbly dough firmly and evenly to the sides and base of an ungreased 9½-inch false-bottom tart pan. Prick the base lightly all over with a fork and refrigerate for at least 20 minutes. Bake the tart crust in the center of a preheated oven, 400°, for about 25 minutes or until the crust is crisp in the center.

While the crust is cooking, make the filling. Put the tomatoes into a bowl, pour boiling water over them and leave them for a few minutes. Drain and peel the tomatoes. Slice each tomato into six or eight slices, depending on size. Put the olive oil into a fairly large, heavy-based saucepan over a medium heat. Add the sliced tomatoes and garlic and cook, stirring often, for about 20 minutes until you have a soft thick mixture. If the tomatoes produce a lot of juice, bubble the mixture at the end to reduce it. Then add the sugar and butter and stir for a few minutes. Remove the pan from the heat and season the mixture to taste with salt and plenty of black pepper. Stir the basil into the tomato mixture. When the crust is ready (if it is ready before the filling, just keep it warm in a low oven), spoon the tomato mixture evenly into it.

If you are using the sage leaves, heat about two tablespoons of olive oil in a skillet over a fairly high heat. Add the sage leaves and toss them around for a few minutes just until they are crisp but not burnt. Put them on to the center of the tart. Put the tart on top of a can or jar and push down the sides. Then, using a spatula, carefully ease the tart off the base of the pan on to a large flat serving plate.

TO SERVE Serve the tart hot or just warm, garnished with the fresh sage and basil leaves, if liked.
Serves 6

SHALLOT AND SCALLION TART WITH CRUNCHY HOT BUTTER PASTRY

This lovely tart can also be served with salad for a light meal. The pastry is easy and does not need to be baked blind.

FOR THE PASTRY:
  1 cup all-purpose flour
  1 cup cream of wheat
  1 teaspoon salt
  1 stick butter
  1 tablespoon water
  1 egg white
FOR THE FILLING:
  1½ pounds shallots
  2 tablespoons olive oil
  1 bunch scallions
  1 large egg
  2 egg yolks
  ½ cup heavy cream
  2 teaspoons superfine sugar
  Salt and black pepper

Mix the flour, cream of wheat and the salt together in a bowl. Gently melt the butter with the water in a small saucepan. Pour the hot butter mixture on to the flour, stirring it in until you have a warm dough. Press pieces of the dough over the bottom and up the sides of an ungreased 10-inch false-bottom fluted tart pan, bringing the edge slightly up above the rim of the pan. Brush the pastry case all over with egg white and place it in the refrigerator while you prepare the filling.

Peel the shallots and slice them across in fairly thin rings. Put the olive oil into a large heavy skillet over a medium heat. Add the shallots and cook, stirring frequently, for about 15 minutes or until the shallots are really soft. If they begin to brown, reduce the heat. Then set the shallots aside to cool a little.

Trim the scallions and slice them across into ¼-inch pieces, using as much of the green part as possible.

Whisk the egg and egg yolks together in a mixing bowl and then whisk in the cream. Season with salt and plenty of black pepper.

Stir the cooled shallots and the chopped scallions into the egg and cream mixture. Pour the mixture into the chilled pastry case. Level the surface of the tart with a knife and sprinkle it with the sugar. Cook the tart towards the top of a preheated oven, 425°, for about 25 minutes or until the tart is just set in the middle and small speckles of black have appeared on the surface. Put the tart pan on to a can or jar and push the sides down carefully. As the pastry is very crumbly, you may find it easiest to place the tart on to a serving plate still on its pan base. However, if you leave it to cool a bit and use a thin spatula, you can carefully ease the pastry off the base.
Serves 8

SUMMER STUFFED ONIONS WITH FRESH MINT, DILL AND PARMESAN CHEESE

With a fresh, herby sauce enveloping the chopped onion and small tender green peas in the center of a soft half-onion shell, these stuffed onions make an appetizing cold first course. You can use other tender fresh herbs in the sauce, or you can use feta cheese instead of Parmesan. It is better not to chill this dish before serving because the flavor is best at room temperature.

  3 large onions
  2 cups small tender green peas
  1 large garlic clove, roughly sliced
  1½ cups mixed fresh mint and dill
  ¼ cup freshly grated Parmesan cheese
  4 tablespoons lemon juice
  ½ cup extra virgin olive oil
  2 teaspoons superfine sugar
  ¼ cup pine nuts, toasted (optional)
  Salt and black pepper
  Whole sprigs of mint and dill, to decorate

◀ Shallot and scallion tart with crunchy hot butter pastry

Place the whole unpeeled onions in a roasting pan and cook them in the center of a preheated oven, 400°, for 45–50 minutes. Remove the pan from the oven and leave the onions to cool. Meanwhile, cook the peas, drain and set them aside. Put the garlic into a food processor with the mint and dill, the Parmesan cheese, lemon juice, olive oil and the sugar. Process until the sauce is as smooth as possible; then season the sauce to taste with a little salt and black pepper.

When the onions are cold, cut off the top and bottom of each with a sharp knife and peel off the skin. Slice the onions in half, crossways, and with a spoon, take out all the soft inside of each onion, leaving the outer shell intact. Brush the outside of the onion with oil. Chop the inside part of the onions into small pieces. Place in a bowl and stir in the toasted pine nuts (if using), peas and the sauce.

TO SERVE Place the onion shells on six individual plates and spoon in the onion, pea and herb mixture, piling it up in the center. Decorate with sprigs of fresh mint and dill. Then spoon a little more olive oil over the top of each onion before serving.
Serves 6

▲ Summer stuffed onions with fresh mint, dill and Parmesan cheese

SUKIE'S SYMPHONY

I made this mixture of briefly steamed squid with ribbons of pink trout on a salsa-type sauce especially for my great friend Sukie. It is a cold dish which you can serve as a first course or a main course.

6–8 ounces small leaf spinach
Juice of 2 lemons
1 large eggplant
12 ounces plum tomatoes
6 tablespoons extra virgin olive oil
8 ounces ready-prepared small
  squid
8–10 ounces pink trout fillets
2 tablespoons sherry vinegar
1 teaspoon superfine sugar
Generous bunch fresh dill, finely
  chopped
Salt
Black pepper

Boil the spinach for about one minute. Drain well. Put the lemon juice into a measuring container, and make it up to 1½ cups with water. Pour the liquid into a saucepan. Peel the eggplant and cut the flesh into small cubes, throwing the cubes into the lemon water as you do so to prevent them from becoming discolored. Cover the saucepan and bring the liquid to the boil. Cook the eggplant cubes for 5–8 minutes or until they are soft and translucent. Drain the eggplant. Put the tomatoes in a bowl and cover with boiling water; then peel them and slice the flesh.

Heat two tablespoons of the extra virgin olive oil in a large saucepan over a medium heat. Add the tomato and cook for one minute. Then add the cooked eggplant and remove the pan from the heat.

Slice the squid across thinly, leaving the tentacles whole. Skin the trout fillets and slice thinly lengthways. Put the squid and trout into the top of a steamer. Steam the fish for about two minutes only, just until the squid is opaque and the trout is a pale pink. Remove the fish from the heat and leave it to one side to cool. Add the sherry vinegar and sugar to the vegetable mixture in the pan. Stir in the remaining olive oil and season the mixture with salt and black pepper. Stir in the chopped dill. Finally, roughly mix in the wilted spinach leaves.

Spoon this mixture into a shallow serving dish and arrange the tangle of squid and trout on top of the sauce. Whether a first or main course, this should be served at room temperature.
Serves 8 as a starter

SHRIMP AND SMOKED HADDOCK MOUSSE WITH SCALLOP SAUCE

This pretty, melt-in-the-mouth mousse can also be served as a main course for four people.

FOR THE MOUSSE:
  1 cup heavy cream
  Generous pinch saffron strands
  1–2 fresh red chilies
  8 ounces cooked, shelled shrimp
  1 pound smoked haddock, roughly
    chopped
  4 large egg whites
  2 egg yolks
  2–3 pinches chili powder
  Salt
FOR THE SAUCE:
  6 fresh scallops
  ¾ stick sweet butter
  1 tablespoon cornstarch
  1 cup milk
  2 egg yolks, lightly whisked
  1–2-inch piece fresh root ginger,
    sliced very thinly
  Generous handful fresh coriander
    leaves, roughly chopped
  3–4 teaspoons sherry vinegar
  Chili powder
  Salt
  Sprig fresh coriander, to garnish

To make the mousse, put the cream and saffron into a saucepan. Bring the mixture to boiling point, then stir and leave to cool, stirring now and then to infuse the saffron.

Meanwhile, cut the chili in half lengthways under running water and remove the seeds and stem. Slice the chili across very thinly. Generously butter a cake pan big enough to take four cups of liquid. Arrange a few shrimp in the center of the cake pan base with one or two slivers of chili among them. When the cream has cooled, put the chopped haddock into a food processor with the egg whites and the two yolks. Process the mixture until just puréed. Then turn it into a mixing bowl, add the saffron cream and the remaining shrimp and stir to mix thoroughly. Season the mixture with the chili powder to taste, and salt if you think it needs it.

Put a roasting pan full of hot water on the center shelf of the oven and heat to 350°. Spoon the mousse mixture into the cake pan and spread level. Put the cake pan into the roasting pan of water and cook the mousse for 25–30

minutes or until firm to touch.

While the mousse is cooking, make the sauce. Slice the scallops. Melt two tablespoons of the butter in a heavy-based saucepan, then remove the pan from the heat, and, using a wooden spoon, stir in the cornstarch until smooth. Gradually stir in the milk. Put the pan back over the heat and bring to the boil, stirring. Allow the mixture to bubble for 2–3 minutes, stirring all the time, until it is thickened and smooth. Then add the whisked egg yolks and the scallop slices and ginger to the sauce. Bubble gently, stirring for a further minute or two, until the scallop slices are opaque. Remove the pan from the heat. Stir in the coriander. Add the sherry vinegar, chili powder and salt to taste.
TO SERVE Loosen the edges of the mousse carefully with a knife and turn it out on to a warmed serving plate. Garnish with a sprig of coriander. Pour the sauce into a warmed bowl.
Serves 6

▶ *Sukie's symphony; shrimp and smoked haddock mousse with scallop sauce*

AVOCADOS IN SPINACH JELLY
WITH GARLIC AND CHILI

This is a refreshingly different way to serve avocado, and it won't discolor even if prepared ahead. Buy firm avocados so they retain their shape when they are peeled and sliced.

1½ cups water
3–4 pinches chili powder
5 spinach leaves, roughly chopped
3 garlic cloves, roughly chopped
4 teaspoons superfine sugar
3 avocados
2 tablespoons white wine vinegar
3 teaspoons powdered gelatin
4 tablespoons lemon juice
Salt
1–2 sprigs fresh dill, to garnish
(optional)

Put the water, chili powder, chopped spinach, garlic, sugar and a good sprinkling of salt into a saucepan. Bring the mixture to the boil and leave to simmer over a gentle heat for about 10 minutes.

Meanwhile, cut the avocados in half lengthways. Remove the pits and peel off the skin, taking as much care as possible not to spoil the shape of the avocado by pressing into the flesh. Cut the avocado flesh across in fairly thin, half-moon slices and put the slices into a bowl, sprinkling them with the white wine vinegar as you do so to prevent them from discoloring. Then arrange the avocado slices in layers in an attractive 4-cup serving dish.

Remove the spinach mixture from the heat, sprinkle in the gelatin powder and stir the mixture until the gelatin powder has dissolved. Then stir in the lemon juice.

Strain the liquid only through a fine strainer into a jug, discarding any spinach and garlic left in the strainer. Immediately pour the strained liquid on to the avocados, slowly so that it seeps right through down to the bottom of the serving dish and between all the slices of avocado. Leave until cool, then refrigerate for at least three hours, or until set. Take out of the refrigerator just before serving. Garnish with the fresh dill, if using.
Serves 6

NEW POTATOES WITH QUAILS' EGGS
AND HERBY CREAM CHEESE MAYONNAISE

Potatoes are one of my favorite ingredients and I quite often use them in a first-course dish. The herby cream cheese mayonnaise is not a mayonnaise in the true sense of the word because it uses no eggs; the light creaminess combined with fresh basil, parsley, extra virgin olive oil and hazelnut oil is lovely. Quails' eggs can usually be found in gourmet shops, but if they are not available, you can use small hens' eggs instead.

1 pound small waxy new potatoes,
* unpeeled*
12 quails' eggs (or 6 small hens'
* eggs)*
FOR THE MAYONNAISE:
* Handful flat leaf parsley*
* 14 fresh basil leaves*
*   (approximately)*
* ½ cup cream cheese*
* 2 tablespoons lemon juice*
* 5 tablespoons extra virgin olive oil*
* 3 tablespoons hazelnut oil*
* Salt*
* Chili powder*

◄ *Avocados in spinach jelly with garlic and chili*

Steam or boil the potatoes until they are cooked, then set aside. Lower the eggs gently into the boiling water, bring the water back to the boil again and boil for 2½–3 minutes (or six minutes for hens' eggs). Drain the eggs and leave them in a bowl of cold water.

To make the mayonnaise, reserve a few perfect leaves of flat leaf parsley for garnishing later and chop the remaining parsley and basil leaves roughly. Put the cream cheese into a food processor with one tablespoon of the lemon juice and process together. Then add the olive and hazelnut oils, a very little of each at a time, processing well between each addition. Process in the remaining tablespoon of lemon juice, season to taste with salt and chili powder and then process in the chopped parsley and basil. If you are not eating this dish immediately, refrigerate the mayonnaise until it is needed.

TO SERVE Shortly before eating, assemble the dish. Peel the eggs and slice both the eggs and potatoes in half lengthways. Arrange the potatoes and eggs together on individual serving plates and spoon some of the herby

cream cheese mayonnaise to one side. Garnish the dish with the reserved whole parsley leaves.
Serves 4

▲ *New potatoes with quails' eggs and herby cream cheese mayonnaise*

PICKLED HERRING AND APPLE IN SOUR CREAM

Try to find herring fillets marinated in a mild, sweet brine for this quick-to-make refreshing first course.

4 pickled herring fillets
1 large firm apple
1 cup sour cream
½ whole nutmeg, grated
1 small red onion, thinly sliced
Handful fresh coriander leaves
Generous handful fresh mint leaves,
* finely chopped*
1 pretty-leaved lettuce
Salt
Chili powder

Rinse the herring fillets thoroughly under running cold water and pat them dry with paper towels. Using a sharp knife, cut the fillets across into thin pieces. Peel the apple, cut it in half, then slice it in very thin half-moon slices. Spoon the sour cream into a mixing bowl and add the grated nutmeg. Season with salt and chili powder to taste, then stir in the sliced herring, the onion and the apple. Reserve a few perfect whole leaves of coriander for garnish and roughly chop up the rest. Stir the chopped mint and coriander leaves into the sour cream

mixture. Cover the bowl and chill the mixture in the refrigerator until you are ready to eat.

Shortly before serving, arrange some pretty lettuce leaves on six individual serving plates. Spoon the herring and sour cream mixture in a pile in the center of each plate.
TO SERVE A perfect accompaniment to this dish is Highland Oatcakes (page 148). Otherwise, serve with the thinnest slices of brown bread or German rye bread. Garnish with the whole coriander leaves.
Serves 6

SMOKED SALMON IN SHRIMP CREAM WITH DILL AND GREEN PEPPERCORNS

This mixture is creamy, though no cream is used, and more delicate than a pâté.

½ stick sweet butter
8 ounces shelled shrimp
½ cup Greek yogurt
¼ whole nutmeg, grated
8 ounces smoked salmon
2 teaspoons green peppercorns
Handful fresh dill, finely chopped
2–4 pinches chili powder
Salt

Melt the butter gently in a small saucepan. Pour the butter into a food processor with the shrimp and the yogurt. Process thoroughly until smooth. Turn the mixture into a mixing bowl and season to taste with the grated nutmeg and chili powder and a little salt. Slice the salmon up into small pieces. Put four rounded teaspoons of the salmon pieces aside, and cover with plastic wrap. Stir the remaining salmon into the puréed

shrimp mixture. Spoon the shrimp mixture into six individual soufflé dishes and chill for several hours in the refrigerator. Before serving, chop the peppercorns finely, mix them with the dill and sprinkle them all over the top of each dish. Lastly, scatter the reserved smoked salmon pieces over each individual dish and serve.
TO SERVE Accompany with thin slivers of toast.
Serves 6

PINK TROUT BALLS WITH DILL VINAIGRETTE

This light dish makes a titillating start to a summer meal.

FOR THE TROUT BALLS:
8–10 ounces pink trout fillets,
* skinned*
3–4 pinches chili powder
Finely grated zest of 1 small lemon
2 tablespoons crème fraîche
1 large egg white
1 small endive lettuce
Salt
Fresh dill, to garnish
FOR THE DILL AND LEMON VINAIGRETTE:
4 tablespoons lemon juice
1 teaspoon superfine sugar
Small bunch dill, finely chopped
¾ cup light olive oil
Sea salt and black pepper

Put the trout into a food processor with the chili powder, lemon zest, crème fraîche and egg white. Sprinkle with a little salt and process until smooth. Turn the mixture into a bowl, cover and refrigerate for about 30 minutes. Then, using dampened hands, take up small amounts of the mixture and roll into balls about the size of a large marble. Bring a large saucepan of salted water to a fierce boil, drop in the balls separately and boil them for 2–3 minutes or until they all rise to the surface. Remove the saucepan from the heat. Using a slotted spoon, remove the balls carefully and put them aside into a bowl to cool. Do not refrigerate.

Meanwhile make the vinaigrette. Put the lemon juice and sugar into a

clean 1-pound jar. Add a little crushed sea salt and black pepper, to taste. Next add the dill and olive oil, cover the jar tightly and shake the vinaigrette thoroughly. Taste for seasoning and add a little more lemon juice to increase the sharpness if you like.
TO SERVE Lay the endive leaves on four individual plates. Arrange the fish balls among the tangle of leaves. Just before serving, shake up the dressing again and spoon a little over each plate. Garnish with fresh dill.
Serves 4

▶ *Pickled herring and apple in sour cream; smoked salmon in shrimp cream with dill and green peppercorns; pink trout balls with dill vinaigrette*

FRESH TOMATO SOUP WITH DICED ZUCCHINI, BASIL LEAVES AND OLIVE OIL

There are few dishes as good as a light and refreshing tomato soup. You can make this soup in advance but add the zucchini only a few minutes before serving. For a completely vegetarian dish, this soup is still excellent without the anchovies.

2½ pounds ripe tomatoes
½ stick butter
1 can anchovies
4 garlic cloves, finely chopped
3 teaspoons superfine sugar
4 cups vegetable stock
1 pound zucchini
10–14 fresh basil leaves, thinly sliced
Extra virgin olive oil
Salt and black pepper

Slit the tops of the tomatoes and put them into a bowl. Pour over enough boiling water to cover and leave them for 1–2 minutes. Then skin the tomatoes, chop the flesh finely and put aside.

Put the butter into a large, heavy saucepan, add the anchovies and their oil and put the pan over a low heat. Stir the mixture until the anchovies dissolve into a purée. Then add the chopped tomatoes and garlic, the sugar and the vegetable stock. (If your tomatoes are not really ripe and deep red, you can add a little tomato paste or sun-dried tomato paste.) Bring the mixture up to the boil and then simmer gently in the open pan, stirring often, for 20–30 minutes until the tomatoes

are completely mushy. Season the soup to taste with black pepper, and salt only if necessary. Put the soup on one side until the meal is nearly ready.

Cut the zucchini into small cubes. To reheat the soup, bring it up to boiling point, add the cubed zucchini and allow the soup to bubble for 1–2 minutes until they are just tender.
TO SERVE Ladle the soup into individual bowls, then add one or two tablespoons of extra virgin olive oil to each bowl and sprinkle the fresh, sliced basil leaves on top. Serve the soup with a plate of thin shavings of fresh Parmesan cheese (you can use a potato peeler for this) and warmed Italian ciabatta bread or rolls.
Serves 6–8

SPICED EGGPLANT AND MINT SOUP WITH CUCUMBER

This is a chilled soup which, for me, is evocative of my young childhood days in the Middle East. The smoky richness of the grilled eggplant is combined with characteristic spices, yogurt and mint – all irresistible flavors. If possible, buy the spices whole and grind them in a coffee grinder or mortar and pestle shortly before using.

2 large or 3 medium eggplants
3 tablespoons olive oil
5 large garlic cloves, halved lengthways
1 rounded teaspoon ground cumin
1 rounded teaspoon ground coriander
1 rounded teaspoon paprika
4 tablespoons lemon juice
2 rounded teaspoons superfine sugar
Generous handful fresh mint leaves
2 cups plain yogurt
1 cucumber, peeled and cubed
Salt
3–5 pinches chili powder
Light cream, to serve
Mint leaves, to garnish

◄ *Fresh tomato soup with diced zucchini, basil leaves and olive oil*

Put the eggplants under the hottest broiler for 10–20 minutes, turning them once or twice until the skins are really blackened and even cracked.

Meanwhile, put the olive oil in a skillet over a low heat. Add the halved garlic cloves and the ground cumin, coriander and paprika and stir just until the garlic has softened – keep the heat low so that it doesn't burn.

Dip the charred eggplants in a sink of cold water so they are cool enough to handle. Scrape out all the flesh of the eggplants into a strainer. Press out as much liquid from the eggplant flesh as you can, using the back of a spoon. Then put the flesh into a food processor with the lemon juice and process to a smooth purée.

Add the fried garlic with its oil and spices, the sugar and the mint leaves to the purée in the food processor. Process until the mint is very finely chopped. Turn the mixture into a mixing bowl and stir in the yogurt. Season to taste with salt and chili powder. Stir the peeled, cubed cucumber into the soup. Put the bowl in the refrigerator to chill well for about 30 minutes.

TO SERVE Serve in individual bowls with a generous swirl of light cream and a small fresh mint leaf to decorate each one.
Serves 6

▲ *Spiced eggplant and mint soup with cucumber*

EMERALD SOUP WITH SCALLOPS AND WATER CHESTNUTS

For a clear scarlet soup, substitute finely chopped raw beets for the spinach.

1 pound spinach
6 cups water
2-inch piece fresh root ginger
4 whole star anise
Coarsely grated zest and strained
*   juice of 1 orange*
2 tablespoons white wine vinegar
12 ounces–1 pound bay scallops or
*   8–10 large ones*
Bunch scallions
7½-ounce can water chestnuts
Salt and black pepper

Remove any thick stems from the spinach. Roughly chop the leaves, then put the spinach, the water and about three teaspoons of salt into a large pan. Cut up the ginger fairly roughly without peeling and add it to the pan, together with the star anise and the orange zest and juice. Bring the mixture to the boil, then cover the pan and simmer gently for 15–20 minutes. Remove the pan from the heat and strain the liquid through a fine strainer into a bowl, pressing the spinach down hard with the back of a wooden spoon to extract all its liquid. Pour the strained liquid back through the strainer into a clean pan. Add the vinegar, season to taste with salt and pepper and leave the pan to one side.

Leave bay scallops whole, if using, but slice larger scallops across thinly. Slice the scallions into ¼-inch pieces, using as much of the green part as possible. Drain the water chestnuts and slice them very thinly. If you aren't going to eat this soup for several hours, put the scallops, scallions and water chestnuts into the refrigerator and cover them with plastic wrap.

Just before serving, bring the saucepan of spinach liquid up to the boil, then reduce the heat so that it is barely bubbling and add the scallops, the scallions and the water chestnuts. Cook the soup very gently for only two minutes, or just until the scallops are opaque and lightly cooked.
TO SERVE Serve immediately while still hot from a warmed tureen with fresh crusty rolls or bread.
Serves 6

CHILLED ZUCCHINI, AVOCADO AND YOGURT SOUP

Here is a tangy, refreshing and easily made soup for lazy summer meals.

1 fresh red chili
3 cups chicken or vegetable stock
1 pound small zucchini, cubed
1 large ripe avocado
4 tablespoons lemon juice
1 cup Greek yogurt
Handful fresh mint leaves, sliced
*   across in thin strips*
Salt and black pepper

Cut the chili open lengthways under cold running water and remove the seeds and stem, then chop the flesh finely. Bring the chicken or vegetable stock to the boil in a saucepan, then add the zucchini and the chili. Cover the pan and simmer for just about three minutes, or until the zucchini are slightly softened but still a bright green. Remove the pan from the heat and, using a slotted spoon, remove the zucchini pieces from the stock and put them aside. Now, cut the avocado in half, remove the pit and scoop out the flesh into a food processor with the lemon juice, yogurt and a little of the stock. Process until smooth, then spoon this purée into the pan with the remaining stock and stir to mix evenly. Season to taste with some salt and black pepper and leave until cold. Stir in the zucchini and the mint.
TO SERVE Pour the soup into a serving bowl and chill well in the refrigerator before serving.
Serves 6

LIMA BEAN SOUP WITH BROILED PEPPERS AND SAUTÉED GARLIC

10 ounces dried lima beans
1 large or 2 small red bell peppers
3 tablespoons sweet butter
2 cups milk
2 tablespoons extra virgin olive oil
2–3 large garlic cloves, thinly sliced
2 tablespoons lemon juice
2–4 pinches chili powder
Salt

◀ *Emerald soup with scallops and water chestnuts; chilled zucchini, avocado and yogurt soup; lima bean soup with broiled peppers and sautéed garlic*

Soak the lima beans in cold water for several hours or overnight. Drain the beans, cover them in fresh unsalted water and simmer over a low heat in a covered pan until they become very soft – about 30 minutes to one hour. Meanwhile, quarter the bell pepper lengthways (or cut into halves if using smaller peppers), discarding the seeds and stem. Lay the pieces skin side upwards under a very hot broiler until they are completely blackened. Place them in a plastic or paper bag until they have cooled slightly, then remove the black skin and cut the peppers into very thin strips. Drain the cooked lima beans, then purée in a food processor together with the butter. Gradually process in the milk and then add chili powder and a little salt to taste. Put the oil into a large saucepan over a fairly high heat, add the garlic and stir for a few minutes until the garlic turns golden brown, but is not burnt. Add the soup to the saucepan and heat. Finally, stir in the lemon juice gradually and add the strips of broiled pepper.
Serves 4–5

PASTA, GRAINS & LEGUMES

Grains and beans are invaluable for giving body and protein to a vegetarian meal, but they are too often abused, with the result that they become stodgy, monotone and formless. This need not be the case, as I hope to prove in this chapter. Combined with carefully cooked vegetables or with chicken and fish you can create something really exciting. For years I found rice extremely boring, but that was before I had experienced the light fluffiness and real flavor of Persian rice, the delicate nuttiness of basmati and Thai fragrant rice and the irresistible texture of a risotto made with arborio rice. Luckily, these kinds of rice are now much more easily available as are many more exotic ingredients and aromatics to combine with them. Dried beans are versatile and satisfying, but age and condition greatly affect their cooking time, so they have to be checked fairly often. The high protein content of beans is a particular bonus for vegetarians. Pasta is, of course, almost everyone's favorite, and it is invariably the answer when you have to produce a last-minute meal. It is such a good and versatile vehicle for other ingredients that there is endless scope for experimenting with Italian or more exotic flavors.

FAVA BEAN, ONION AND SAFFRON RISOTTO

Before I had tasted a real risotto, I had no idea of its wonderful creaminess and subtle texture. It relies not only on the rice, which should be the Italian arborio or similar variety, but also on a really fine home-made stock. Whenever I have made chicken stock, I make risotto. For vegetarians, a good fresh vegetable stock is also successful.

> 5 cups home-made chicken or
>   vegetable stock
> Generous pinch saffron strands
> Generous ½ stick sweet butter
> 4 tablespoons olive oil
> 2 large onions, chopped
> 5 large garlic cloves, finely chopped
> 1 pound risotto rice
> 1 pound frozen fava beans
> Salt and black pepper

◄ *Fava bean, onion and saffron risotto*

Put the chicken or vegetable stock into a saucepan, add the saffron and bring the stock to the boil. Remove the stock from the heat and leave it for at least 15 minutes, stirring occasionally to infuse the saffron. Put the stock back over a low heat.

Melt ½ stick of the butter with the olive oil in a large saucepan over a fairly low heat. Add the chopped onion and stir until the onion is soft and translucent, but not browned. Then add the chopped garlic and stir the mixture for one minute. Next add the rice and stir for about two minutes. Pour in about ½ cup of the hot stock and bring it to simmering point. Using a wooden spoon, stir the rice continuously until it has absorbed all the stock, then add a little more stock.

Continue like this, adding a little more stock each time the stock has been absorbed, stirring all the time. It will probably take about 30 minutes to cook the rice to the point where it is soft but still has a slight bite to it.

Shortly before all the stock has been added to the rice, bring a saucepan of salted water to the boil. Cook the fava beans for 2–3 minutes only and then drain through a strainer.

Add the fava beans to the risotto after you have added the last of the stock. Finally, stir in the remaining butter and season to taste with salt, if necessary, and plenty of black pepper. Turn the risotto into a heated serving dish and eat without delay.

TO SERVE Serve with a chunk of Parmesan cheese to grate freshly on to each serving. Risotto can be eaten simply on its own, or accompanied by a green salad if you wish.

Serves 6

SMOKED HADDOCK AND MUSHROOM LASAGNE WITH CRUNCHY ALMOND TOP

Lasagne is useful for large families or for parties as it can be prepared well ahead and then cooked when you are ready. Use fresh lasagne if available.

8 ounces oven-ready lasagne sheets
* or fresh lasagne*
1 pound skinned smoked haddock
* fillets or other smoked white fish*
½ stick butter
2 large garlic cloves, finely chopped
½ nutmeg, grated
½ cup all-purpose flour
1 cup plain yogurt
3 cups milk
2 cups grated cheese
10–12 sun-dried tomatoes, thinly
* sliced*
6 ounces chestnut mushrooms,
* thinly sliced*
Generous handful of parsley,
* roughly chopped*
¾ cup slivered almonds
Grated Parmesan, for sprinkling
Salt and black pepper

If you are using oven-ready lasagne, it cooks better if first soaked for 10–15 minutes in a sink filled with hot water and a little cooking oil. Then remove the sheets and lay them out separately on a clean cloth to drain. Steam the fish for 2–3 minutes only and leave on one side. Melt the butter in a fairly large saucepan over a medium heat. Add the garlic and the grated nutmeg and stir for 30 seconds. Remove the saucepan from the heat and stir in the flour until smooth. Then stir in the yogurt. Return the pan to the heat and stir in one direction only until the mixture starts to bubble. Now add the milk gradually, stirring all the time, and increase the heat until the mixture comes to the boil. Simmer the mixture, still stirring, for 2–3 minutes until it is slightly thickened. Then add the grated cheese and stir until the cheese has melted. Remove from the heat and season to taste, but do not add more salt if your fish is already salty.

Pour a little more than 1 cup of the sauce into a measuring jug and reserve it for the top. Then flake the fish into the remaining sauce in the pan and stir in the prepared sun-dried tomatoes, mushrooms and parsley. Generously butter a large, ovenproof gratinée dish and arrange a layer of the lasagne sheets on the bottom. Cover these sheets with a layer of the sauce, then arrange another layer of the lasagne sheets over the sauce. Repeat this process, ending with a layer of lasagne. Then spread the reserved cheese sauce over the top of the lasagne and scatter the slivered almonds evenly on top. Finally, sprinkle the top liberally with grated Parmesan cheese.

When you are ready to cook, bake the lasagne in the center of a preheated oven, 350°, for 35–40 minutes or until the top is a rich golden brown.
TO SERVE This is best served with a simple salad or just as it is.
Serves 8

CANNELLONI STUFFED WITH SPINACH IN WHITE WINE AND GRUYÈRE SAUCE

Lighter than most cannelloni dishes, this is good as a main course or a starter, and can easily be prepared in advance.

2 pounds spinach
Finely grated zest and juice of
* 1 orange*
1 cup milk
10 strands saffron
16 oven-ready cannelloni tubes
½ stick butter
1 large garlic clove, finely chopped
¼ cup all-purpose flour
1½ cups dry white wine
5 ounces Gruyère or Emmental
* cheese, coarsely grated*
2 egg yolks
4–5 pinches chili powder
Salt and black pepper

Either boil or steam the spinach leaves until they are just soft. Drain the spinach thoroughly and then press out all the excess moisture using double thicknesses of paper towels. Put the

leaves into a bowl and stir in the orange zest and a sprinkling of salt and black pepper. Put the milk and saffron into a small saucepan. Bring the milk up to bubbling, remove from the heat and leave aside, stirring now and then to infuse the saffron into the milk.

Meanwhile, fill the cannelloni tubes as follows: using your hands, roll bits of the spinach into sausages of the same length as the cannelloni tubes but thinner. Hold a cannelloni tube upright and insert the sausage of spinach into it, pressing it in gently with the end of a thin-handled wooden spoon if necessary. Repeat this process with all the cannelloni tubes. When all the tubes are filled, lay them out neatly in a rectangular ovenproof gratinée dish.

Melt the butter in a saucepan over a medium heat. Add the chopped garlic and stir for 30 seconds. Remove the pan from the heat and stir in the flour until smooth. Now gradually stir in the milk and saffron, the white wine and

the orange juice. Put the pan back over the heat and bring to the boil, stirring all the time. Stir for about three minutes, keeping it bubbling, until it has thickened to the consistency of heavy cream. Add all but two tablespoons of the grated Gruyère or Emmental cheese and stir until it has melted. Then remove the pan from the heat and whisk in the egg yolks. Finally, season to taste with salt and chili powder and pour the sauce all over the cannelloni in the dish. Sprinkle the top evenly with the reserved cheese. When you are ready to cook, place the dish just above the center of a preheated oven, 375°, for 35 minutes or until the top is a rich golden brown. Serve immediately.
Serves 4

▶ *Smoked haddock and mushroom lasagne with crunchy almond top; cannelloni stuffed with spinach in white wine and Gruyère sauce*

BASMATI RICE COOKED IN WHITE WINE AND SAFFRON WITH SALMON

This rice dish does not have the smooth creaminess of a risotto, which should always be made with arborio, or a similar type rice, and the gradual addition of a really good home-made stock. But basmati, India's king of rice, has supreme flavor, texture and lightness. You can also use Thai fragrant rice for this recipe.

1¼ cups basmati rice
2 generous pinches saffron strands
5–6 pinches chili powder
Generous 1 cup dry or medium sweet white wine
50g (2oz) butter
2½-pound piece salmon (unfilleted weight), filleted and skinned
1 bunch fresh chives, chopped
Generous handful fresh dill, chopped
Generous handful flat leaf parsley, chopped
Sea salt

Put the rice into a strainer and wash thoroughly with running cold water. Then put the rice into a bowl with two cups of cold salted water and soak for at least one hour.

Meanwhile, put the saffron strands into a separate bowl together with a generous sprinkling of sea salt and the chili powder. Put the wine into a saucepan. Bring the wine up to boiling point and then pour it into the bowl with the saffron and seasoning. Leave the saffron for the same length of time as you soak the rice, stirring once or twice to infuse the saffron strands.

Put the butter in a saucepan and melt it over a medium heat. Drain the rice through a sieve and stir it into the butter in the pan. Then add the wine and saffron mixture. Bring the mixture up to bubbling, cover the pan immediately with a well-fitting lid and turn the heat down to as low as you possibly can. Cook the rice for 10–14

minutes only until it is tender but still has a slight bite to it.

While the rice is cooking, cook the salmon. If the rice is ready a bit before the fish, turn off the heat, put a cloth between the cover and the saucepan and leave it in a warm place. To cook the salmon, simply put it in the top of a covered steamer over boiling water for 5–10 minutes – it depends on the thickness of the fillet – until the salmon is lightly cooked, but still grading to a slightly darker pink in the center. Then flake the fish into a mixing bowl.

When the rice is ready, turn it into the mixing bowl with the salmon and, using a large fork, mix together thoroughly. Season if necessary with more salt and chili powder. Stir in the chopped herbs.
TO SERVE Turn the rice into the warmed serving dish and serve at once with a green salad.
Serves 4–5

GARLIC AND GREEN LENTIL RISOTTO

In Gujurat, the staple dish is *kichri*, a mixture of rice and lentils, which was the original inspiration for kedgeree. Here I have combined an Italian-style risotto with lentils, and flavored it with an Indian mixture of herbs and spices.

4–4½ cups chicken or vegetable stock
1–2 fresh red chilies
Generous ½ stick sweet butter
8 large garlic cloves, halved lengthways
2-inch piece fresh root ginger, chopped finely
4–5 cardamom pods, lightly crushed
2 teaspoons cumin seeds
1½ cups risotto rice (arborio)
¾ cup green or brown lentils, washed through in cold water
Handful fresh coriander leaves, chopped roughly
Salt

◄ *Basmati rice cooked in white wine and saffron with salmon*

Bring the stock up to the boil in a saucepan, and allow it to simmer gently throughout the making of your risotto. Cut the chilies open under running water, discard the seeds and stem and slice very finely across.

Melt ½ stick of the butter in a large, heavy-based saucepan over a low heat. Add the garlic and stir until the garlic is soft, translucent and golden brown. Stir in the chopped ginger, the sliced chilies, the crushed cardamom pods and the cumin seeds. Then add the rice and lentils and stir for about two minutes. Next pour in about ½ cup of the simmering stock and stir constantly with a wooden spoon over a medium heat until the rice and lentils have absorbed all the stock. Add a little more simmering stock and stir until it has also been absorbed.

Continue like this until the rice is soft but still has a slight bite to it. If all the stock has been absorbed before the rice is ready, you can add a little boiling water. Finally, stir in the

remaining butter and add salt if necessary. Serve on a warm serving dish, sprinkled with the coriander.
Serves 4

▲ *Garlic and green lentil risotto*

CABBAGE LEAVES STUFFED WITH RED BEANS AND HERBY TOMATOES

This simple dish is both aromatic and piquant: the scented flavor of rosemary contrasts with a bite of chili and ginger. It can be served as an accompaniment or main dish, with good bread to mop up the juices.

1½ cups dried red kidney beans
1¼–1½ pounds loosely packed green cabbage
2 sprigs fresh rosemary
8 ounces tomatoes
½-inch piece fresh root ginger, finely chopped
3 large garlic cloves, very finely chopped
1 rounded teaspoon paprika
1 tablespoon tomato paste
1 large egg
2 tablespoons lemon juice
½ cup chicken or vegetable stock
1 fresh red chili
Sea salt
2–3 pinches chili powder

Soak the kidney beans in plenty of cold water for at least eight hours or overnight; then drain the beans. Put them in a saucepan and cover them with unsalted water. Boil the beans rapidly for 10 minutes, then reduce the heat and simmer gently until they are just soft but not so soft they break up. Drain the beans in a colander and rinse through with cold water to cool them. Put the beans into a mixing bowl. Bring a saucepan of salted water to the boil. Separate the cabbage leaves and boil them in the salted water for two minutes until they are limp. Drain the leaves and lay them out on a flat surface.

Take the leaves off one of the rosemary sprigs and chop them finely. Put the tomatoes in a bowl and pour boiling water over to cover them. Leave the tomatoes for two minutes, then drain, skin and chop them. Add the tomatoes to the kidney beans together with the ginger, garlic, chopped

rosemary, paprika and tomato paste. Season well with sea salt and chili powder and mix thoroughly with a wooden spoon. Finally, whisk the egg lightly then stir it into the beans.

Butter a large shallow casserole dish. Spoon the bean mixture in compact piles on to each cabbage leaf and bring up the leaves to enclose the beans completely. Carefully place the cabbage bundles, with the beans underneath, in the casserole. Pour the lemon juice and stock over them. Break the remaining sprig of rosemary into pieces and place them in the stock among the cabbage packets. Cut the chili open lengthways under running water, discard the seeds and stem and slice the flesh across very thinly. Scatter the chili over the cabbage packets and cover the casserole. Cook the dish in the center of a preheated oven, 350°, for 45 minutes–1 hour.
Serves 6

TOMATOES STUFFED WITH CRACKED WHEAT, PEAS AND CHUTNEY

These juicy stuffed tomatoes, packed with flavor, are delicious eaten either hot or cold as a first course or for a light meal, accompanied by crusty bread and a green salad. They are very simple and quick to prepare.

4 very large tomatoes
1 cup cracked wheat (bulgar)
6 ounces frozen small peas
3 tablespoons olive oil
3 large garlic cloves, very finely chopped
1 small sprig fresh rosemary, very finely chopped
2 rounded tablespoons tomato chutney
Generous handful roughly chopped small mint leaves
Olive oil, for brushing
Salt
Black pepper

◀ *Cabbage leaves stuffed with red beans and herby tomatoes*

Slice just the tops off the tomatoes and set aside. Using a small spoon, scoop out all the seeds and most of the flesh and chop the flesh into small pieces. Lightly salt the insides of the tomato shells and lay them upside down in a colander to drain away the excess liquid. Put the cracked wheat into a bowl and cover with water. Put the frozen peas in a strainer and rinse with cold water just to defrost them.

Put the oil into a large skillet over a fairly high heat and add the chopped tomato flesh, garlic and rosemary. Allow the mixture to bubble, stirring all the time, for about five minutes until well-reduced and thickened. Remove the pan from the heat and stir in the chutney. Drain the cracked wheat through a strainer and press out any excess moisture. Then stir the wheat into the tomato mixture together with the mint and peas. Season to taste with salt and black pepper.

Rinse the salt from the tomato shells and dry them with paper towels. Put

the shells into a shallow ovenproof dish. Spoon the cracked wheat and pea mixture into the hollow tomato shells and then balance the reserved tomato tops on top.

Brush the stuffed tomatoes all over with olive oil. Cook the tomatoes in the center of a preheated oven, 350°, for 20–30 minutes, or until they are soft.
Serves 4

▲ *Tomatoes stuffed with cracked wheat, peas and chutney*

PASTA SHELLS WITH SMOKED OYSTERS AND QUICK-FRIED SPINACH

This simple, instant dinner dish is nevertheless excellent. You can use smoked mussels instead of oysters if you like, or a mixture of both. If you have one, a wok is even better for this than a skillet.

12 ounces small spinach leaves
2 x 3-ounce cans smoked oysters or
*   smoked mussels*
8–10 ounces pasta shells
½ cup extra virgin olive oil
3 large garlic cloves, finely chopped
Salt and black pepper
Grated Parmesan, to serve
*   (optional)*

First prepare the ingredients. Wash and drain the spinach and then shake it in a cloth to dry it as much as possible. Then, if necessary, take the stalks off the spinach and cut up the leaves unless they are really small. Open the cans of oysters so that they are ready to use. Then bring a large pan of salted water to boil, drop in the pasta shells and cook them for 7–12 minutes until they are *al dente* – just cooked but still with a very slight bite to them. As soon as you have put the water on to boil, you should start cooking the other ingredients. Put the olive oil into a large, deep skillet over a high heat. When the oil is very hot, add the chopped garlic followed by the spinach leaves. Stir swiftly for barely one minute, just until the spinach has become limp. Lastly, stir in the smoked oysters and their oil. Remove the pan from the heat and season with plenty of black pepper and a little salt if needed. When the pasta is ready, drain and put the pasta into a heated serving bowl. Pour the skillet mixture on top and lightly mix in the pasta. Serve immediately, with grated Parmesan.
Serves 4

CHICKEN AND SPINACH PASTA PIE

A pasta pie has two main advantages: not only is it a dish that can be put together quickly at the last minute, but it can also be prepared ahead of time to avoid any last-minute panics. Pasta and chicken are both universally popular, so a combination of the two is always a useful family dish. This pasta pie can simply be cooked and then reheated, or it can be left in the refrigerator, after you have spooned the sauce on top and sprinkled it with grated cheese, until you are ready to cook it. When you can find them, the extra-wide flat ribbon noodles are especially good for this dish, but the ordinary tagliatelle is also suitable.

1 pound spinach
4 ounces wide noodles (tagliatelle
*   or wider)*
1–1¼ pounds boneless, skinless
*   chicken thighs*
2 tablespoons olive oil
2 large garlic cloves, finely chopped
1 rounded tablespoon tomato paste
3–4 pinches chili powder
¼ stick butter
2 rounded teaspoons ground mace
¼ cup all-purpose flour
2 cups milk
¾ cup grated Cheddar cheese
Salt and black pepper

◄ *Pasta shells with smoked oysters and quick-fried spinach*

Bring a saucepan of salted water to the boil, add the spinach and boil the leaves for only a few minutes or until they are just limp. Drain the spinach and press out all the excess moisture using the back of a spoon. Set aside. Bring a large saucepan of salted water to the boil, add the pasta and cook it until the pasta is *al dente* – just cooked but still with a slight bite to it. Drain the pasta and mix in a very little olive oil to prevent it sticking together. Keep the pasta aside in a bowl.

Using a sharp knife, cut the chicken up into very small pieces. Put the olive oil into a large heavy skillet over a fairly high heat. Add the chicken pieces and stir for 2–3 minutes, then add the chopped garlic and the tomato paste. Turn the heat down a little and continue stirring for a further three minutes. Remove the pan from the heat and season the chicken to taste with salt and the chili powder. Then transfer the mixture to a large, shallow ovenproof dish and spread the top level. Cover the chicken evenly with the cooked spinach.

Melt the butter in a saucepan. Stir in the mace and remove the pan from the heat. Then stir in the flour until the mixture is smooth. Gradually stir in the milk and return the pan to the heat. Bring the mixture to the boil, stirring all the time, and then allow it to bubble, still stirring, for about three minutes until the sauce is thickened and smooth. Remove the pan from the heat and season to taste with salt and black pepper.

Pour half the sauce into the ovenproof dish over the spinach leaves. Then spread the cooked noodles over the sauce and spoon the remaining sauce on top. Finally, sprinkle the top with the grated cheese. Cook the pie just above the center of a preheated oven, 400°, for 25–35 minutes or until it is a rich, golden brown.
TO SERVE Serve with a crisp green salad or a mixed salad.
Serves 6

▲ *Chicken and spinach pasta pie*

TAGLIATELLE WITH ARUGULA, ORANGE ZEST AND HAZELNUT OIL

Arugula, orange zest and hazelnut oil is a perfect combination, making this one of the simplest, but most delicious, pastas.

Zest of 1 orange
8 ounces tagliatelle
4 tablespoons hazelnut oil
2 tablespoons extra virgin olive oil
3 generous handfuls arugula leaves
Salt and black pepper

Put a serving bowl in a low oven to keep warm. Bring a large saucepan of salted water to the boil. Meanwhile, remove the zest from the orange in thin strips with a zester, or alternatively, grate the zest coarsely. When the water is boiling, add the tagliatelle and the orange zest and cook until the pasta is *al dente* – still with a slight bite to it. Drain the pasta and return it to the empty saucepan. Stir in the hazelnut oil and olive oil. Season the pasta with salt and plenty of black pepper and lastly stir in the arugula leaves.

TO SERVE Turn the pasta into the warm serving bowl. Put a bowl of thinly shaved or freshly grated Parmesan cheese on the table to scatter on top of the pasta. Eat at once.
Serves 4

SPAGHETTI WITH PEAS, SCALLIONS AND PEA, MINT AND SOUR CREAM SAUCE

A simple dish tasting of summer, this is perfect for a light lunch on a hot day. I find that the best fresh peas are those you know have only just been picked, as they become rather starchy within a day of harvesting. However, frozen very small peas work extremely well for this recipe. You can use tagliatelle or another type of pasta instead of spaghetti if you prefer.

1 pound fresh or frozen peas
Generous handful mint leaves
1 cup sour cream
2 tablespoons extra virgin olive oil
1 bunch scallions
10 ounces spaghetti
Salt and black pepper
Fresh mint leaves, to garnish

Bring a large saucepan of salted water to the boil. Add the frozen peas and boil for two minutes. If using fresh peas, boil for five minutes. Then drain the peas and put one-third of them into a food processor with the mint leaves, the sour cream and the olive oil. Process the mixture to a purée. Then put the mixture into a bowl and season to taste with salt and plenty of black pepper. Add the remaining whole peas and cover the bowl with foil. Put the sauce into a very low oven, together with another bowl suitable for serving the pasta, to keep warm while you are cooking the spaghetti.

Bring a large saucepan of salted water to the boil. While it is coming to the boil, slice the scallions across into ¼-inch pieces, using as much of the green part as possible. When the water is boiling, put in the spaghetti and boil it for 7–10 minutes (perhaps less if you are using fresh pasta) or until it is *al dente* – just cooked, but still with a slight bite to it. Drain the spaghetti into a colander and rinse with running hot water. Then put the spaghetti into the warmed serving bowl. Stir the sliced scallions into the sauce, then mix the sauce roughly into the pasta.

TO SERVE Garnish with fresh mint leaves and serve at once accompanied by a bowl of freshly grated Parmesan cheese, or fine slivers of Parmesan shaved from a whole piece of cheese with a potato peeler.
Serves 4

SPAGHETTI WITH PECANS, PARSLEY, BASIL AND RED CHILI

This quick, delicious pasta dish is also good with chopped walnuts instead of pecans, but walnuts do have a rather stronger taste.

½ cup shelled pecans
2 red chilies
5 tablespoons extra virgin olive oil
1–2 large garlic cloves, chopped
*   finely*
Generous handful flat leaf parsley,
*   finely chopped*
3 tablespoons very hot water
10–14 fresh basil leaves, thinly
*   sliced*
8 ounces spaghetti
Salt

Put a serving bowl in a low oven to keep it warm. Put the pecans into a food processor and grind them only roughly. Cut open the chilies under running water, remove the seeds and stem and then slice the chilies across very finely.

Put two tablespoons of the olive oil in a saucepan over a low heat. Add the garlic, chili and parsley to the pan and stir for 30 seconds. Add the ground nuts and stir around for about one minute, being careful not to let them brown. Then stir in the remaining three tablespoons of olive oil and the hot water. Season the mixture with salt and remove the saucepan from the heat.

Add the sliced basil leaves to the pecan mixture in the pan.

Bring a large pan of salted water to the boil, add the spaghetti and cook until the pasta is *al dente* – just cooked, but still with a slight bite to it.

When it is ready, drain the pasta, put it into the warmed serving bowl and stir in the pecan mixture thoroughly. Serve immediately.
Serves 4

► *Tagliatelle with arugula, orange zest and hazelnut oil; spaghetti with peas, scallions and pea, mint and sour cream sauce; spaghetti with pecans, parsley, basil and red chili*

LIMA BEANS WITH SMOKY ZUCCHINI PURÉE

When using dried beans, remember that older beans need longer cooking.

8 ounces dried lima beans
2 large sprigs fresh rosemary
8–10 fresh bay leaves
1 pound ripe plum tomatoes
Scant ½ stick butter
2 teaspoons chopped fresh rosemary
2 teaspoons golden superfine sugar
1 pound zucchini
2 tablespoons plain yogurt
Olive oil, for brushing
Salt and black pepper

Soak the beans overnight. Drain them and bring them to the boil in fresh, unsalted water with the rosemary sprigs and bay leaves. Simmer gently for 20–40 minutes until just soft right through.

Meanwhile, cover the tomatoes with boiling water for two minutes, then drain, peel, and halve them lengthways. Melt the butter in a sauté pan over a medium heat and add the tomatoes and the chopped fresh rosemary. Stir the tomatoes gently for about five minutes. Then stir in the sugar and remove the pan from the heat. When the beans are ready, remove the herbs, drain the beans and put them in a serving bowl. Stir in the tomato mixture and season to taste. Keep warm.

Trim the zucchini and halve lengthways. Smear them with olive oil and sprinkle with salt on both sides, then broil them, skin side upwards, until the skin has blackened. Purée them together with the plain yogurt. Season to taste and serve with the lima beans and tomato mixture.
Serves 4

CANNELLINI BEANS WITH LEMONY DILL SAUCE

This delicate creamy sauce spiked with lemon and fresh dill is lovely either with cannellini or haricot beans.

6 ounces dried cannellini beans
2 tablespoons olive oil
FOR THE SAUCE:
½ cup heavy cream
Finely grated zest and juice of 1 lemon
Handful fresh dill, finely chopped
Salt and black pepper

Soak the beans in cold water overnight. Then drain them and put them into a saucepan with plenty of unsalted water. Bring the beans to the boil and simmer for 30–50 minutes (older beans will take longer) until they are soft but not breaking up.

Drain the beans, and put them into a warm serving bowl. Stir in the olive oil, and keep the beans in a warm place while you make the sauce.

To make the sauce, put the cream and the lemon zest into a saucepan. Bring to the boil and bubble, stirring, for two minutes. Then remove the pan from the heat and gradually stir in the lemon juice, followed by the chopped dill. Season to taste with salt and plenty of black pepper. Mix the sauce into the cooked beans and serve immediately for a light meal with bread or salad.
Serves 4

LENTIL TART WITH RICE CRUNCH PASTRY

This delicious crumbly tart is highly reminiscent of traditional English vegetarian fare and is perfect for a homey informal meal.

FOR THE PASTRY:
1½ cups all-purpose flour
1 teaspoon salt
¼ cup cream of wheat
1 stick butter
1 tablespoon water
FOR THE LENTIL FILLING:
1 onion, finely chopped
1 cup orange lentils
2 cups milk
1 teaspoon ground mace
3–5 pinches chili powder
1 large egg
½ cup grated Cheddar cheese
Paprika, to sprinkle
Salt

To make the pastry, sift the flour and salt into a bowl and stir in the cream of wheat. Put the butter and water in a saucepan and melt the butter gently. Then pour the melted butter into the flour mixture, stirring it in with a wooden spoon to form a warm dough. Press this dough evenly over the base and sides of a 9-inch false-bottom tart pan, bringing it up slightly above the rim of the pan. Refrigerate the pastry while you make the filling.

Put the chopped onion into a saucepan with the lentils and the milk. Simmer very gently in the open pan for 45 minutes–1 hour, stirring now and then, until the mixture is thick and mushy. Stir in the ground mace and season to taste with salt and chili powder. Leave until cool. Then whisk the egg in a bowl and stir it into the cooled lentil mixture. Spoon the lentil mixture into the pastry-lined pan and sprinkle the grated cheese on top. Lastly, sprinkle the top sparingly with paprika. Cook the tart in the center of a preheated oven, 375°, for 35–45 minutes or until the filling has set.

Remove the tart from the oven and leave it in the pan for a few minutes. Then push up the tart out of the pan sides very carefully. Using a long wide spatula, ease the tart off the base of the pan on to a flat, round serving plate.
TO SERVE Serve with fresh tomato sauce made with juicy ripe tomatoes and a mixed, crisp salad.
Serves 4–5

▶ Lima beans with smokey zucchini purée; cannellini beans with lemony dill sauce; lentil tart with rice crunch pastry

EGGS & CHEESE

During my early childhood, for no very good reason, I decided I didn't like eggs. Luckily, the first omelet I tasted on a vacation in France made me realize how silly I had been. Soon after that I picked up a new-laid egg from my grandmother's hen hutch and she poached it for me; I had to admit that I had never tasted anything quite so good as that light and creamy-textured white with the orange yolk running over it. I cannot imagine where I would be without eggs; what would life be like without the cakes, omelets, soufflés, real vanilla ice creams, mayonnaise, sauces and all the other miracles that eggs produce in the kitchen? Eggs provide a richness of flavor and wide variation of textures. The yolks can make sauces satin-smooth while thickening them to just the right degree and the fluffy lightness of the whites make a mixture rise to astonishing heights. Cheese, equally versatile, combines naturally with eggs and enhances many other ingredients. Leafy salads and green vegetables are at their most irresistible when speckled with thinly shaved or grated Parmesan. Vegetables with a gratin of melted cheese on top are always welcome. In fact, cheese dishes are the most popular choice for light but nutritious meals and snacks.

CAULIFLOWER CHEESE WITH SUN-DRIED TOMATOES, FRESH RED CHILI AND CRUNCHY PARMESAN TOPPING

I have never grown out of a fondness for good English nursery food, although all too often it is rather bland. Not so, however, with this more sophisticated version of an old favorite.

1 large cauliflower
1 fresh green chili
8–10 sun-dried tomatoes
½ stick butter
2 garlic cloves, finely chopped
2 tablespoons all-purpose flour
2 cups milk
1 cup plain yogurt
1½ cups grated cheese (pecorino or Cheddar)
FOR THE TOPPING:
2 tablespoons white breadcrumbs
1 tablespoon grated Parmesan
2 tablespoons olive oil
Salt and black pepper

◄ *Cauliflower cheese with sun-dried tomatoes, fresh red chili and crunchy Parmesan topping*

Break up the cauliflower into medium-sized florets. Either boil or steam the florets until they are just soft. Drain and arrange the cauliflower in a large, fairly shallow ovenproof dish.

Cut open the chili lengthways under running water, discard the seeds and stem and then chop the chili finely. Slice the sun-dried tomatoes. Melt the butter gently in a large saucepan over a medium heat. Add the garlic to the melted butter in the pan and stir around with a wooden spoon for about one minute. Then remove the saucepan from the heat. Stir in the chopped chili and the sun-dried tomatoes. Then stir in the flour until the mixture is smooth. Gradually stir in the milk, a little at a time, followed by the yogurt.

Return the saucepan to the heat and bring the mixture to the boil, stirring it in one direction only (this prevents the yogurt curdling) until the mixture thickens. Allow the mixture to bubble, still stirring all the time, for 2–3 minutes. Then add the grated Cheddar or pecorino cheese and stir until the cheese has melted.

Remove the saucepan from the heat. Season the sauce to taste with a little salt (the cheese adds a certain saltiness to the sauce anyway) and black pepper and then pour it over the cauliflower in the ovenproof dish.

To make the topping, put the breadcrumbs into a bowl and stir in the grated Parmesan cheese and olive oil. Mix together thoroughly and season with black pepper.

Sprinkle the topping mixture evenly over the sauce and cauliflower. Put the cauliflower cheese under a preheated broiler until the top is nicely browned. If you are not quite ready to eat, you can keep this dish warm in a low oven for up to 30 minutes. Serve warm.
TO SERVE This can be served as a main dish or as an accompaniment to broiled chicken or fish.
Serves 4 as a main dish

THREE-CHEESE CUSTARD

This delicious baked egg custard is topped with a rich cheese and chive sauce and makes an excellent lunch or dinner dish.

FOR THE CUSTARD:
- *4 large eggs*
- *2 cups milk*
- *2 ounces mature Cheddar cheese, finely grated*
- *½ teaspoon freshly grated nutmeg*
- *Salt and black pepper*

FOR THE SAUCE:
- *½ stick butter*
- *¼ cup all-purpose flour*
- *1 cup milk*
- *3 ounces Gruyère or Emmental cheese, grated*
- *1 egg yolk*
- *3 pinches chili powder*
- *2 rounded tablespoons fresh chives, chopped*
- *½ cup Parmesan cheese, grated*

Half-fill a roasting pan with water and place it in the center of the oven. Set the oven to preheat at 300°.

While the oven is heating, make the custard. Break the eggs into a mixing bowl and whisk lightly. Heat the milk in a saucepan to just below boiling point and stir in the Cheddar cheese until melted. Remove the pan from the heat and whisk the hot milk into the eggs, a little at a time. Whisk in the grated nutmeg and season well with salt and black pepper. Pour the custard mixture into a buttered round 4-cup ovenproof dish. Place the dish in the roasting pan of water and bake for 1¼ to 1½ hours, or until the custard feels firm to a light touch in the center. If the custard begins to brown during cooking, cover it loosely with foil.

While the custard is cooking, make the sauce. Melt the butter in a saucepan over a low heat, remove the pan from the heat and stir in the flour using a wooden spoon. Gradually stir in the milk, then place the saucepan back on the heat and bring the mixture to the boil, stirring all the time. Reduce the heat and simmer for 2–3 minutes, stirring constantly.

Remove the sauce from the heat and stir in the Gruyère or Emmental cheese. When the cheese has melted, stir in the egg yolk thoroughly, then season with the chili powder and salt to taste and stir in the chopped chives. Finally, pour the sauce gradually over the custard and sprinkle generously with the Parmesan cheese. Place the custard under a medium broiler until the top is golden brown in patches, and serve immediately.

TO SERVE Serve accompanied by a green salad and warm crusty bread or Tomato, Herb, Parmesan & Garlic Bread (see page 151).
Serves 4

CHEESE, SPINACH AND SORREL ROULADE

If you can't get sorrel for this pretty roulade, try substituting arugula or a mixture of spinach and watercress.

- *2 tablespoons Parmesan cheese, finely grated*
- *¾ pound fresh spinach, finely chopped*
- *Handful sorrel leaves*
- *1 cup fresh white breadcrumbs*
- *6 ounces mature Cheddar cheese, finely grated*
- *4 large eggs, separated*
- *½ cup light cream*
- *3–4 pinches chili powder*
- *3 rounded tablespoons cottage cheese*
- *3 teaspoons bottled green peppercorns*
- *Salt*
- *Salad leaves, to garnish*

Line a 9 x 13-inch jelly roll pan with a piece of buttered waxed paper and sprinkle it evenly with half the grated Parmesan cheese. Place the chopped spinach in a saucepan with very little salted water, cover and cook for 3–5 minutes or until the spinach is soft. Drain the leaves and then press them between double layers of paper towels to dry thoroughly; then leave them on one side. Slice the sorrel leaves into very thin strips and leave them separately on one side.

Mix the breadcrumbs and grated Cheddar cheese together in a mixing bowl. Using a wooden spoon, stir in the egg yolks, cream and the sliced sorrel leaves. Season the mixture with salt and chili powder to taste. In a separate bowl, add a pinch of salt to the egg whites and whisk until they stand in soft peaks; then, using a metal spoon, fold them gently into the cheese mixture. Pour the cheese and egg mixture into the prepared pan and bake in the center of a preheated oven, 400°, for 10–15 minutes or until the roulade has risen and is firm to a light touch in the middle. Remove the roulade from the oven and leave to cool in the pan – it will shrink slightly. Sprinkle a little water over a clean towel to dampen it, lay it on top of the roulade and leave until completely cold.

Meanwhile, drain the cottage cheese in a sieve and place it in a bowl. Stir in the spinach. Crush the green peppercorns roughly with a pestle and mortar and add them to the mixture, together with a little salt to taste. When the roulade is cold, sprinkle a sheet of waxed paper slightly larger than the roulade all over with the remaining grated Parmesan. Remove the towel from the roulade, loosen the edges with a knife and turn the roulade out on to the waxed paper. Spread the roulade evenly with the cheese and spinach mixture and then roll it up fairly loosely with the help of the paper to form a jelly roll.

TO SERVE Cut the roulade into eight slices with a sharp knife and serve them on individual plates. Garnish each slice with a few salad leaves.
Serves 8

▶ *Three-cheese custard; cheese, spinach and sorrel roulade*

DEEP-FRIED FETA CHEESE AND MUSHROOMS IN BEER AND CARAWAY BATTER

You can use this lovely batter for frying all sorts of raw vegetables to make light crisp fritters, which can then be served either as a first course or as an accompaniment to a main dish. The beer makes the batter lighter and crispier.

1 cup self-raising flour
1 teaspoon salt
½ teaspoon chili powder
2 teaspoons caraway seeds
1 small egg
½ cup dark beer
8 ounces feta cheese
Flour, for coating
8 ounces button mushrooms
Oil for deep frying

Sift the flour, salt and chili powder into a food processor. Then add the caraway seeds and the egg. Process the mixture briefly together; then gradually add the beer, processing between each addition. When all the beer has been incorporated into the batter mixture, pour it into a large bowl and leave it to one side for at least 20 minutes.

Meanwhile, cut the feta cheese into 1-inch cubes and roll each cube in flour to coat it. Slice the mushrooms in half lengthways unless they are very small.

Heat a large pan of oil suitable for deep frying over a high heat until the oil is smoking – peanut oil is a good choice. Put the prepared feta cheese and mushrooms into the bowl of batter and stir the pieces around to coat them thoroughly. Spoon up separate batter-coated pieces of feta or mushroom and put them into the hot oil in batches. Deep-fry the pieces until the batter is golden and crisp. Remove the pieces from the pan carefully with a slotted spoon and place them on paper towels to drain.

TO SERVE As soon as all the pieces are cooked, pile them up on a bed of leaves arranged on a pretty serving dish or on four individual plates. Serve the fritters immediately while they are still warm.

Serves 4

PUFFED RICOTTA AND GORGONZOLA ROLL WITH SUN-DRIED TOMATOES

This delicious crispy and soft roll, with a mixture of Italian cheeses, is easy to make and excellent for a light lunch or dinner. If you prefer, you can prepare it several hours in advance, keep it in the refrigerator and then simply put it in the oven to cook it fresh. If you can get the sun-dried tomatoes sold in jars of oil, they are nice and soft, and their flavor is wonderful with rich, strong cheeses, such as Gorgonzola. As an alternative, you can use grated mature pecorino or any other strongly-flavored cheese.

8 ounces puff pastry
8 ounces ricotta cheese
6 ounces Gorgonzola cheese or
    strongly-flavored Italian cheese
8 sun-dried tomatoes
    (approximately), thinly sliced
10 fresh basil or sage leaves
    (approximately), sliced in strips
1 egg
1 egg yolk
Salt and black pepper
Grated Parmesan cheese, to sprinkle
Fresh basil or sage leaves, to
    garnish

◄ *Deep-fried feta cheese and mushrooms in beer and caraway batter*

Roll the pastry out on a flat surface into a rectangle about 8 x 10 inches. Prick the pastry all over with a fork. Put the ricotta cheese into a bowl and crumble in the Gorgonzola. Add the sliced sun-dried tomatoes and the sage or basil leaves. Whisk the egg lightly in a cup and add to the cheese in the bowl. Season the cheese mixture with a little salt and plenty of black pepper and mix together with a wooden spoon.

Spread the mixture on to the pastry within ½ inch of the edges. Moisten the edges and then roll the pastry up loosely. Press the ends lightly together to seal in the filling. Transfer the pastry carefully to a greased baking tray. If you are not ready to cook the pastry roll at once, put it in the refrigerator until it is needed.

When you are ready to cook it, brush the roll all over with the egg yolk; then make slanting slashes with a sharp knife along the top at 1-inch intervals. Sprinkle the roll lightly with the grated Parmesan cheese.

Sprinkle the baking tray with a little water all around the roll (but do not dampen the roll itself). Cook the roll on a high shelf of a preheated oven, 425°, for 20–30 minutes, or until the pastry has risen and is a rich golden brown and puffy all over.

TO SERVE Garnish the roll with the fresh basil or sage leaves.

Serves 4

▲ *Puffed ricotta and Gorgonzola roll with sun-dried tomatoes*

DEVONIAN SPANISH OMELET

Every summer in England, we have a picnic beside the River Dart in Devon, and we always have this thick Spanish omelet, packed with good things. Served warm or cold, it is delicious.

1 large red bell pepper
1 large yellow bell pepper
12 ounces onions
2 small garlic cloves
2 tablespoons olive oil
¼ stick butter
10 ounces firm-textured potatoes,
  boiled and cubed
10 sun-dried tomatoes, thinly sliced
10 large eggs
¾ cup coarsely grated cheese or
  ½ cup grated Parmesan cheese
2 handfuls fresh mixed herbs,
  including dill, roughly chopped
Salt and black pepper

Cut open the red and yellow bell peppers lengthways and remove the seeds and stem. Slice the onions finely. Chop the garlic finely. Put the olive oil and butter into a large, deep, heavy-based skillet – about 10 inches in diameter – over a fairly low heat. Add the garlic to the pan and cook gently for one minute. Add the sliced onions and continue to cook gently, stirring around occasionally. Meanwhile, put the peppers, skin side upwards, under a very hot broiler until the skin has blackened. Remove the peppers, and put them into a paper bag until they are cool enough to handle. Then peel off the skin and slice thinly.

When the onions are really soft but not browned, add the cubed potatoes, the sliced peppers and the sliced sun-dried tomatoes. Stir to mix and remove from the heat. Break the eggs into a bowl and whisk together lightly. Stir in the grated cheese and chopped herbs and a good seasoning of salt and black pepper. Pour this mixture into the skillet of ingredients, stir once and return the pan to a low heat. Cook for about 15 minutes until all but the central part is set; then cover the pan with foil and continue cooking for a few more minutes until the omelet is set to a light touch in the center. If you want, you can put the skillet under a broiler to brown the top.

TO SERVE Cut the omelet like a cake straight from the pan. If you are taking this on a picnic, take it along still in the pan you cooked it in, wrapped in waxed paper and layers of newspaper to keep it hot.
Serves 6–8

EGG, CHEESE AND ONION GRATIN WITH CHERRY TOMATOES

Cheese dishes are always popular with children and adults alike, and this is one of those soothing, family dinner dishes which everybody will welcome after a tiring day. Fresh sage and cheese combine particularly well, and the whole cherry tomatoes add a fresh juiciness. It could be accompanied by any number of things, but you can serve it with a green vegetable, such as steamed broccoli, or with a salad, and waxy-textured new potatoes are also very good.

8 large eggs
8 ounces cherry tomatoes
10 fresh sage leaves
  (approximately), chopped
Generous ½ stick butter
¼ whole nutmeg, grated
½ cup all-purpose flour
1½ cups milk
1 cup strong-flavored grated cheese
4–5 pinches chili powder
2 large onions
Salt
Chives, to garnish

Semi-hard boil the eggs (7–8 minutes from the time you lower them into the boiling water). Cool in a sink of cold water; then peel and cut them across in thick slices. Put the egg slices on the bottom of a fairly shallow ovenproof dish. Arrange the cherry tomatoes among the slices of egg. Scatter the chopped sage over the top.

Melt ½ stick of the butter in a heavy-based saucepan over a medium heat. Remove the pan from the heat and stir in the nutmeg. Then stir in the flour until the mixture is smooth. Gradually add the milk, stirring all the time. Put the pan back over the heat and bring the mixture to the boil. Bubble gently, still stirring, for 2–3 minutes until the sauce is thick and smooth. Then add the grated cheese and stir until melted. Remove the pan from the heat and season to taste with salt and the chili powder.

Slice the onions across thinly in rings. Melt the remaining butter in a heavy-based skillet and fry the onion rings over a fairly high heat until soft and golden brown. Then stir the onions into the cheese sauce mixture. Spoon the sauce over the eggs and tomatoes in the ovenproof dish.

Place the dish near the top of a preheated oven, 400°, and bake for 20–30 minutes or until the top of the gratin has turned a rich golden brown. Serve garnished with chives.
Serves 4–5

▲ *Egg, cheese and onion gratin with cherry tomatoes*

◀ *Devonian Spanish omelet*

OVEN-BAKED PANCAKE ROLLED WITH GOATS' CHEESE, TOMATOES AND BASIL

The taste of melting hot goats' cheese is, to me, a really supreme gastronomic pleasure. One day, I developed this dish entirely for my own satisfaction. The yellow cherry tomatoes look especially pretty in the filling.

FOR THE PANCAKE BATTER:
  4 tablespoons olive oil
  Generous ¼ cup all-purpose flour
  1 large egg
  ½ cup milk
FOR THE FILLING:
  1 egg
  11 ounces soft fresh goats' cheese
  8–10 basil leaves
  3 ounces yellow or red cherry
    tomatoes
  2 tablespoons olive oil
  Grated Parmesan cheese, to sprinkle
  Salt and black pepper

To make the batter, simply put all the ingredients in a food processor with a generous pinch of salt and process thoroughly until the mixture is completely smooth. Generously butter a 13 x 9-inch roasting pan. Put the pan on the top shelf of a preheated oven, 475°, for a few minutes to heat up. Then pour the batter into the hot pan, put the pan back in the oven and cook for 10 minutes or until the batter is risen and golden. Remove the pan from the oven. Turn the cooked batter out on to a flat surface and cover it with a clean and slightly damp cloth.

For the filling, put the egg into a bowl and whisk lightly. Then add the soft goats' cheese and mix the egg and cheese together thoroughly with a wooden spoon. Slice the basil leaves thinly across and add them to the egg and cheese mixture. Season the filling with salt and plenty of freshly ground black pepper. Lastly, cut the cherry tomatoes in half, and fold them into the cheese mixture.

Remove the cloth from the pancake. Spread the filling mixture evenly all over the pancake and then roll it up loosely, from the short end, like a jelly roll. Oil a shallow, rectangular ovenproof dish and lay the roll carefully in it, join side down. Smear the top of the roll with plenty of olive oil and sprinkle generously with grated Parmesan cheese.

Cook the pancake in the center of a preheated oven, 350°, for 20–25 minutes and serve immediately.
TO SERVE Serve with a simple green salad with a vinaigrette dressing.
Serves 4

SOFT GOATS' CHEESE SOUFFLÉS ON A FRESH TOMATO BASE

These individual soufflés make a practical hot first course as they can be prepared in advance, up to the point before you fold in the whisked egg whites, and then freshly cooked minutes before serving. Cooked goats' cheese is always delicious, especially here with a hint of oregano and juicy tomatoes underneath.

  6 ripe tomatoes
  2 teaspoons superfine sugar
  5 ounces fresh soft goats' cheese
  1 teaspoon cornstarch
  3 large eggs
  ½ teaspoon dried oregano
  Grated Parmesan cheese, to sprinkle
  Salt and black pepper

Butter six deep individual soufflé dishes, spreading the butter generously on the bottom and more thinly up the sides. Put the tomatoes in a bowl, pour boiling water over to cover them, and leave them for 1–2 minutes. Drain, peel and chop the tomatoes very finely and put the pieces back into the bowl,

◄ Oven-baked pancake rolled with goats' cheese, tomatoes and basil

including any juices. Stir in the superfine sugar and a good seasoning of salt and black pepper. Divide the tomato mixture evenly between the six buttered dishes.

Put the soft goats' cheese into a bowl. Add the cornstarch and mix it in thoroughly with a wooden spoon. Separate two of the eggs (putting the whites into a large, clean bowl) and mix the yolks into the cheese mixture until the mixture is very smooth. Stir in the oregano and season well with salt and freshly ground black pepper.

Just before you are ready to eat, put the prepared soufflé dishes together on a baking tray. Separate the remaining egg and add the egg white to the reserved egg white (the yolk can be used in another dish). Add half a teaspoon of salt. Whisk the egg whites until they stand in soft peaks. Then, using a metal spoon, fold them gently into the cheese mixture. Spoon the cheese mixture into the buttered dishes on top of the tomato base and sprinkle the surface lightly with grated Parmesan cheese. Bake the soufflés in the center of a preheated oven, 400°,

for 10–12 minutes or until they are well risen and nicely browned. Serve as soon as they come out of the oven.
Serves 6

▲ Soft goats' cheese soufflés on a fresh tomato base

BILLOWED EGGS BAKED ON RADICCHIO

This is a different way of preparing eggs; the whisked whites set in a soft froth around the yolks.

> 3 tablespoons olive oil
> 12 ounces–1 pound radicchio,
>   roughly sliced
> 4 large eggs
> FOR THE SAUCE:
> ¼ stick butter
> 2 tablespoons all-purpose flour
> 1 cup milk
> 2 teaspoons dried oregano
> Generous ½ cup grated Cheddar
>   cheese
> 4 teaspoons wholegrain mustard
> Chili powder
> Salt

Put the olive oil into a large, deep skillet over a medium heat. Add the sliced radicchio and stir for a few minutes until the leaves are just soft. Spread the leaves on the bottom of a lightly buttered, shallow ovenproof dish and set aside.

To make the sauce, melt the butter in the saucepan, remove the pan from the heat and sift in the flour, stirring until smooth. Gradually add the milk, stirring continuously, and then add the oregano. Return the pan to the heat and bring the sauce to the boil, stirring all the time. Simmer, still stirring, for about three minutes. Then add the grated cheese and the mustard and stir until the cheese has melted. Lastly, add salt and chili powder to taste. Remove the pan from the heat, cover and leave it in a warm place.

Carefully separate the eggs, putting the whole yolks in one bowl and putting the whites into a separate bowl. Add a pinch of salt to the egg whites and whisk until they stand in soft peaks. Spoon the whites into the dish all over the radicchio. Make four holes in the whisked egg white and gently slide a yolk into each. Bake just above the center of a preheated oven, 425°, for 7–10 minutes, or until the yolks are just softly set. Serve at once, pouring the cheese sauce around the eggs.

TO SERVE Serve with toast and salad.
Serves 4

HARD-BOILED EGGS IN CURRIED SAUCE

Here is a recipe which tastes delicious and home-made, but is so easy and quick to make it seems like cheating.

> 8 large eggs
> Large handful fresh coriander
>   leaves
> 6 ounces ricotta
> 2–3 teaspoons mild curry paste
> 2 tablespoons Greek yogurt
> Salt

Semi-hard boil the eggs for eight minutes from the time the water returns to the boil after adding the eggs. Drain the eggs and put them into a sink of cold water to cool slightly before peeling and halving lengthways. Arrange the halves in a warmed, shallow serving dish. Remove eight small sprigs of coriander and chop up the remainder as finely as possible. Put the ricotta into a saucepan over a fairly low heat, and, using a wooden spoon, stir in two teaspoons of the curry paste. Then stir in the yogurt until the mixture is smooth. Finally stir in the finely chopped coriander and season the sauce with salt to taste. Add another teaspoonful of curry paste if you think the sauce needs it. Spoon the sauce over the egg halves and garnish with the reserved coriander.

Serves 6

EGGS POACHED ON A BED OF ONIONS AND ENDIVE

Onions are sweet, and endive has a subtle bitterness, and this combined with a mild bite of chili tastes excellent in this simple dish. Serve with good crusty bread to mop up the delicious juices.

> 3 large endives
> 1 fresh red or green chili
> ½ stick butter
> ½ cup vegetable stock
> 4 onions, sliced in thin rings
> 2 teaspoons superfine sugar
> Generous handful flat leaf parsley,
>   roughly chopped
> 4 large eggs
> Salt
> Chili powder

Cut off the bases of the endives and cut them across in ½-inch pieces. Cut the chili open under running water, discard the seeds and stem and then slice the flesh across thinly. Melt the butter in a large skillet over a medium heat, then pour in the stock. Add the onions to the pan and cook for 4–5 minutes. Then add the endive and the chili. Allow the mixture to bubble gently over a low heat until the vegetables are soft. If all the liquid is not evaporated by the time the vegetables are ready, increase the heat and continue to bubble until no liquid is left. Then stir in the sugar and cook for one minute. Remove the pan from the heat. Season the mixture to taste with salt and chili powder. Stir the chopped flat leaf parsley into the onion and endive mixture. Then level the mixture in the pan, and, using a spoon, make four hollows in it. Break an egg into each hollow.

Now cover the skillet with a cover or a piece of foil and put it back over a fairly low heat for 3–5 minutes or until the whites of the eggs have set – don't allow the egg yolks to become at all hard. Serve straight from the pan.

Serves 4

▶ *Billowed eggs baked on radicchio; hard-boiled eggs in curried sauce; eggs poached on a bed of onions and endive*

VEGETABLE SIDE DISHES

This chapter is far removed from the accompanying vegetable dishes which you might have had in many British or American homes 30 years ago. We have come to appreciate vegetables far more in recent years; a much greater variety are available and we have learned to cook them properly. We have also realized from foreign travel and cuisines that instead of serving, for example, separate bowls of unseasoned vegetables and plain boiled potatoes simply as accompaniments to the main dish, vegetables can be combined both with each other and with herbs, spices, interesting oils or other aromatic seasonings to become a much more important part of the meal. Three or four contrasting dishes taken from this chapter, served together, would make a satisfying vegetarian meal, or they can be served with a main course of chicken or fish. Mixing vegetables together when they have been cooked in different ways can produce an exciting combination of textures and often looks decorative too. The fact that vegetables are so varied in taste, form and texture, and that they contain flavors ranging from stimulatingly bitter to softly sweet has made this one of the most pleasurable chapters to work on. It has left me feeling that I want to try out all sorts of other combinations.

SAUTÉED MUSHROOMS AND BROCCOLI WITH GARLIC AND CORIANDER SEEDS

This simple but delicious mixture is very lightly and quickly cooked so that the broccoli remains slightly crunchy. It can be served either as one of several vegetable dishes to make up a varied vegetarian meal, or served as an accompaniment to broiled chicken or fish.

8 ounces broccoli
4 tablespoons olive oil
2 large garlic cloves
1 teaspoon coriander seeds
8 ounces button or other firm
  mushrooms
Salt
Black pepper

◄ *Sautéed mushrooms and broccoli with garlic and coriander seeds*

Cut any thick stalks off the broccoli and peel and cut them into fairly thin pieces. Divide the broccoli spears into medium-sized florets. Steam or boil both the florets and the sliced stalks until they are just soft but still retain their bright green color. As soon as the broccoli is cooked, submerge it in cold water to stop the cooking process, then drain the broccoli through a strainer when cold.

Put the olive oil in a sauté pan over a medium heat. Chop the garlic cloves as finely as possible. Grind the coriander seeds in a pestle and mortar (or, alternatively, place them in a small plastic bag, such as a freezer bag, or in an envelope, and crush them with a rolling pin or mallet). Using a sharp knife, slice the mushrooms into approximately ¼-inch slices. Add the crushed coriander seeds and the sliced mushrooms to the oil in the sauté pan and stir around until the mushrooms are just soft.

Then add the finely chopped garlic to the mixture and continue to stir for one minute. Lastly, add the drained broccoli to the pan and stir for a further 30 seconds. Remove the sauté pan from the heat and season the broccoli and mushroom mixture with salt and plenty of black pepper.

TO SERVE Turn the mixture into a heated serving bowl to serve hot, although this dish is just as good served at room temperature.

Serves 4

PARSNIPS WITH SHIITAKE MUSHROOMS IN MUSTARD SAUCE

This can be served as a side dish or as a vegetarian main course with salad.

1½ pounds parsnips
6 tablespoons olive oil
6 shiitake mushrooms
Seasoned flour, for coating
FOR THE SAUCE:
¼ stick butter
1 tablespoon cornstarch
1 cup milk
1 teaspoon white wine vinegar
2 teaspoons wholegrain mustard
2 tablespoons plain yogurt
Generous handful parsley, finely
*   chopped*
Salt and black pepper

Trim the parsnips and slice them across into ¼-inch rounds. Steam or boil them until they are just tender. Pat the parsnips dry with paper towels and then dip them into a little seasoned flour. Put the olive oil into a large skillet over a medium heat and sauté the parsnip slices until they are golden brown all over, adding a little more olive oil if you think it necessary. Using a slotted spatula, transfer the parsnips slices to a wide, shallow serving dish, reserving the oil in the pan. Keep the parsnip slices warm in a very low oven.

Thinly slice the shiitake mushrooms. Add them to the reserved oil in the skillet, and stir around for 3–4 minutes, or until they are just soft. Add the mushrooms to the parsnip slices in the oven.

Finally, to make the sauce, melt the butter in a saucepan over a moderate heat and stir in the cornstarch until smooth. Slowly stir in the milk, bring the mixture to the boil and allow it to bubble for about three minutes, stirring all the time. Add the vinegar, mustard and the yogurt and season to taste.

Lastly, stir in the chopped fresh parsley and pour the sauce over the parsnip mixture in the serving dish just before taking it to the table.
Serves 4 as a side dish

SLICED BRUSSELS SPROUTS WITH GARLIC AND CARAWAY SEEDS

One can get very bored with whole, boiled brussels sprouts but they do taste good. Here they are thinly sliced and cooked in butter and a little water.

1½–1¾ pounds brussels sprouts
¾ stick sweet butter
½ cup water
2 garlic cloves, finely chopped
½ teaspoon caraway seeds
Salt and black pepper

Cut off the bases of the brussels sprouts and remove any loose or damaged outer leaves. Then slice them across thinly lengthways. Put the sweet butter and water into a saucepan over a medium heat. When the butter has melted and the mixture is bubbling, add the brussels sprouts. Cover the pan and simmer for 3–4 minutes or until the brussels sprouts are bright green and soft when pierced with a fork.

Then remove the pan cover and add the chopped garlic and caraway seeds. Stir the brussels sprouts around in the open pan for 1–2 minutes or until all the water has evaporated.

Season with salt and pepper and spoon the mixture on to a serving dish.
TO SERVE This dish goes particularly well with plainly roasted poultry or game birds.
Serves 6

BRAISED RED CABBAGE WITH CHESTNUTS AND PEAS

This dish is a perfect accompaniment if you are serving game birds, but it can also be served very successfully on its own as a light meal.

1¾–2 pounds red cabbage
1 cup chicken or vegetable stock
½ stick butter
4 tablespoons sherry vinegar
2 teaspoons dill seeds
3 teaspoons dried green
*   peppercorns*
2 rounded tablespoons redcurrant
*   jelly*
1 pound frozen small peas
14 ounces vacuum-packed chestnuts
Salt
Black pepper

Cut the red cabbage in half, remove the core, and slice into smallish pieces. Put the stock, butter and vinegar into a casserole or heavy-based saucepan and place the pan over a medium heat.

When the butter has melted, add the dill seeds, the peppercorns and the sliced cabbage. Stir to mix thoroughly; then bring the liquid up to boiling point, cover the dish and lower the heat to simmer very gently for 30–40 minutes or until the red cabbage is really soft and mushy.

Add the redcurrant jelly to the cabbage and stir until the jelly has melted. Then add the frozen peas. Bring the cabbage to the boil again and bubble fiercely in the open pan for a few minutes until the juices have almost evaporated. Finally, season the cabbage to taste with salt and pepper and gently stir in the whole chestnuts. Cover the pan and leave it over a low heat for a few minutes before serving so that the chestnuts warm through.
TO SERVE If there are no accompanying dishes, I add more chestnuts to this, or sometimes garbanzo beans instead. Then all it needs is some warm crusty bread.
Serves 6–8

▶ *Parsnips with shiitake mushrooms in mustard sauce; sliced brussels sprouts with garlic and caraway seeds; braised red cabbage with chestnuts and peas*

HERBED SWEET POTATO AND ONION GRATINÉE

Check the color of the potato flesh by scraping away a little skin; they all have the same chestnut-like flavor, but the orange-fleshed ones are far prettier.

4 tablespoons olive oil
3 large onions, finely chopped
3 large garlic cloves, finely chopped
8 ounces sweet potatoes
2 generous sprigs rosemary, finely chopped
10 fresh sage leaves (approximately), finely chopped
Handful parsley, finely chopped
Salt and black pepper

Put the olive oil into a large sauté pan over a medium heat. Add the chopped onion and stir until soft and browned. Then add the finely chopped garlic cloves and stir for another 2–3 minutes. Remove the sauté pan from the heat and turn the onion and garlic mixture into a large mixing bowl.

Peel the sweet potatoes and cut them into large pieces. Put the pieces through the grating blade of a food processor. Turn the grated potato into the bowl with the onion mixture.

Add the chopped rosemary and sage to the bowl and, using a wooden spoon, mix all the ingredients together thoroughly. Season the mixture generously with salt and black pepper. Then spread the mixture evenly into a shallow round or rectangular ovenproof dish. Dribble a little olive oil all over the top of the sweet potato mixture and cook just above the center of a preheated oven, 350°, for about one hour or until the dish is golden brown and crispy on top.

TO SERVE Sprinkle the chopped parsley over the top of the gratinée and serve immediately.

Serves 6

TUSCAN FAVA BEANS

It's useful to have pantry ideas and, although made with frozen beans and canned tomatoes, this is delicious.

19-ounce can chopped tomatoes
½ stick butter
2–3 large garlic cloves, chopped
1 pound frozen fava beans
Black pepper

Put the tomatoes in a heavy saucepan and add the butter and garlic. Season generously with black pepper. Bring the mixture to the boil and add the fava beans. Bring the mixture to the boil again, then simmer in the open pan for 15–20 minutes or until the sauce has reduced and thickened and the liquid has evaporated.

TO SERVE Serve as an accompaniment to a piece of strongly-flavored broiled fish, such as swordfish or tuna, or perhaps with simply roasted chicken or duck. If you prefer, and you have the fresh ingredients, this can be made with fresh fava beans and peeled fresh plum tomatoes.

Serves 5–6

BAKED SANDWICHED EGGPLANTS

These soft baked eggplants are split and sandwiched with a paste of almonds, mint, garlic and black olives. They go well with simple chicken or vegetable dishes.

½ cup blanched almonds
2 large garlic cloves, sliced
Generous handful fresh mint leaves
3 tablespoons black olive paste
1 tablespoon tomato paste
1 egg white
4 small eggplants
2 tablespoons olive oil
Salt and black pepper
Sprigs flat leaf parsley, to garnish

◄ *Herbed sweet potato and onion gratinée; Tuscan fava beans; baked sandwiched eggplants*

Put a dry skillet over a fairly high heat. Add the blanched almonds and stir them around over the heat for one or two minutes, just until they turn brown. Reserve eight of the whole almonds and put the remainder into the bowl of a food processor. Process the almonds until they are very finely chopped. Add the sliced garlic to the almonds in the processor together with the mint leaves and process again thoroughly until the mixture is as smooth as possible. Add the black olive paste, the tomato paste and the egg white. Season the mixture with salt and plenty of black pepper and process once again until the paste is very smooth.

Cut the eggplants in half lengthways and smear the skin with a little olive oil. Spread the cut sides of the eggplants with the almond, mint and black olive mixture and then sandwich the halves back together again. Arrange the eggplants in a shallow ovenproof dish, fitting them closely together so that they can't fall apart. Scatter the reserved whole almonds randomly over the eggplants. Dribble a little more olive oil over them and then cover the dish with foil.

Place the covered dish in the center of a preheated oven, 350°, and cook for 45–60 minutes, removing the foil for the last 20 minutes of cooking time. When the eggplants are fully cooked, they should feel very soft when you stick a small sharp knife into them.

TO SERVE Before serving, garnish the eggplants with flat leaf parsley.

Serves 4

DRIED FAVA BEAN PURÉE WITH GREEN VEGETABLES

This is a well-known dish from the southern Italian region of Apulia. Here food epitomizes the 'Mediterranean' diet, concentrating mainly on vegetables, grains, olive oil and fish. Although it is so simple, this is a star dish. In Italy they use one of their many different varieties of endive as the vegetable to go with this purée – long dark green stems with leaves looking like a smaller arugula. If you cannot find the dried fava beans, you can use dried lima beans as a substitute, but if you do, you should rub them through a strainer after you have cooked them to remove their tougher skins before you start to make the purée.

8 ounces dried peeled fava beans
6 ounces potatoes, peeled
12 ounces collards
2 endives
5 tablespoons extra virgin olive oil
  (approximately)
Sea salt and black pepper

Cover the fava beans with cold water in a bowl, and soak them for one hour or more. Drain the beans in a strainer and put them into a casserole or heavy saucepan. Cut the peeled potatoes into fairly thick slices and lay them evenly on top of the beans. Pour in enough cold water to come about two inches above the level of the potatoes. Don't add any salt at this stage. Bring the water to the boil, remove any scum from the surface of the water with a large spoon, then cover the pan and simmer the potatoes gently for two hours. Check the beans once or twice during cooking and add a little more boiling water if necessary. By the end of cooking, the water should be almost totally absorbed.

While the beans are cooking, prepare the vegetables. Slice the collard leaves across fairly thinly. Cut the base off the endives and slice lengthways in quarters or in thirds, depending on the size of your endives.

When the beans are ready, beat the beans and potatoes together vigorously with a fork to turn it to a purée, beating in the extra virgin olive oil to taste as you do so. Season the mixture to taste with salt and pepper and then turn the mixture into a wide, warmed, serving dish. Cover the dish loosely with foil and place it in a very low oven to keep warm while you cook the vegetables.

To cook the vegetables, bring a large pan of salted water to the boil, add the sliced collards and endive and boil them for about 15 minutes, or until both the collards and the endive are soft. Drain the vegetables and put them on top of the bean purée towards the middle. Sprinkle the dish with sea salt and pepper and dribble some more extra virgin olive oil all over.
TO SERVE The purée can either be served on its own or as an accompanying vegetable to a dish of simply prepared chicken or fish.
Serves 4 as a side dish

NEW POTATOES WITH ANCHOVY AND CHIVE CREAM

The combination of potatoes and anchovies has long been appreciated, but in this creamy, appetizing sauce, flavored with chives, I feel it has rarely been better. This dish goes well with almost anything. Potatoes with a good waxy texture are by far the best to use for this recipe. If you cannot get chives, substitute a little of the green top part of a scallion, but chop it very finely as the flavor is stronger than chives. The dish can be served hot or cold.

1½ pounds new potatoes
2-ounce can anchovies in olive oil
½ cup heavy cream
2 tablespoons plain yogurt
Generous bunch fresh chives, finely
  chopped
Black pepper

◄ *Dried fava bean purée with green vegetables*

Wash the potatoes and scrub off as much of the skin as you can but do not peel them. Cut any larger potatoes in half. Either steam or boil the potatoes until they are cooked and transfer them to a mixing bowl.

Meanwhile, empty the anchovies and their oil into the top of a double boiler or into a bowl set over a saucepan of simmering water. Stir constantly until the anchovies melt down into a smooth mixture. Put the cream into a saucepan, bring it to the boil and bubble the cream for 3–4 minutes until it thickens slightly, stirring all the time. Remove the cream from the heat and stir in the smooth anchovy mixture. Leave to cool. Then stir in the yogurt and season to taste with black pepper – salt shouldn't be necessary because of the salty anchovies. Lastly, stir the chopped chives into the creamy mixture. Then

pour the creamy mixture into the bowl of potatoes. Mix them well together.
Serves 6

▲ *New potatoes with anchovy and chive cream*

RED BELL PEPPER, BABY CARROTS AND ZUCCHINI COOKED IN OLIVE OIL

This is simply a delicious and very pretty and colorful combination of vegetables and different textures. If available, buy the tiny red bell peppers which look like fresh chilies, and get the smallest, youngest spinach leaves you can find.

8 ounces small spinach leaves,
*   trimmed*
1 pound small red bell peppers or
*   2 large red bell peppers*
12 ounces baby carrots
1 pound small zucchini
½ cup olive oil
Sea salt and black pepper

Wash and dry the spinach leaves and lay them in a large shallow serving dish, breaking up any slightly larger leaves. If you are using the tiny bell peppers, simply cut off the stem ends. Otherwise, cut the bell peppers in half lengthways, remove the seeds and stem and slice the flesh across in ½-inch pieces. Cut off the ends of the carrots and slice any larger ones in half lengthways. Trim the zucchini, cut in half across and then slice each half downwards in thin slices.

Put the olive oil into a wide casserole over a fairly gentle heat. Add the prepared peppers and carrots and season with sea salt and plenty of black pepper. Cover the casserole and cook gently for 20–30 minutes or until the peppers are very soft and the carrots are tender. Then stir in the sliced zucchini. Cover the casserole and cook for 8–10 minutes until the zucchini are soft, but still retain their bright green color.

Just before serving, empty the casserole ingredients together with all the olive oil and juices on to the bed of spinach leaves.
TO SERVE This goes well with any piece of poultry or fish.
Serves 6

SAUTÉED LEEKS WITH PUMPKIN SEEDS AND STEAMED SNOW PEAS

I much prefer using snow peas for this dish, but sugar snap peas can be used if snow peas are not available.

6–8 ounces snow peas
¼ stick butter
3 tablespoons olive oil
1 pound leeks, thinly sliced in rings
¼ cup pumpkin seeds
Salt and black pepper

Pinch off the ends of the peas and put them on one side.

Melt the butter with the olive oil in a deep sauté pan over a medium heat. Add the prepared leeks and the pumpkin seeds and stir often until the leeks are soft but not browned. Season with salt and plenty of black pepper. Meanwhile, bring a saucepan of salted water to the boil, add the prepared peas and boil for a few minutes until they are just soft and still bright green. Drain the peas and mix them in with the leeks. Turn the mixture into a heated serving dish.
TO SERVE Like the dish above, this simple combination could be served as a vegetable side dish or as part of a varied vegetarian meal.
Serves 4

SAUTÉED JERUSALEM ARTICHOKE WITH BOK CHOY

The subtle flavor of jerusalem artichokes is brought out in this dish.

1 pound jerusalem artichokes
½ bok choy (root end)
1 fresh red chili
½ stick butter
2 tablespoons sunflower oil
1 tablespoon sesame oil
2 large garlic cloves, finely chopped
2 handfuls flat leaf parsley, chopped
Soy sauce, to sprinkle
Salt and black pepper

◄ *Red bell pepper, baby carrots and zucchini cooked in olive oil; sautéed leeks with pumpkin seeds and steamed snow peas; sautéed jerusalem artichoke with bok choy*

If you are unable to get jerusalem artichokes, small turnips can be used very successfully, and if you cannot get bok choy, savoy cabbage makes an excellent substitute.

Wash and scrub the jerusalem artichokes very thoroughly but don't peel them. Then slice the artichokes across in thin slices. Cut just the base off the bok choy, then slice it across very thinly. Cut the chili open lengthways under running water, discard the seeds and stem and then slice the flesh across as thinly as you possibly can.

Put the butter and both the sunflower and sesame oils in a wok or a large, deep skillet over a fairly high heat. Add the slices of artichoke and toss them around in the skillet with a large spoon for 3–4 minutes until they are softened but still slightly crunchy and holding their shape. Then add the chopped garlic and chili and the sliced bok choy. Stir this mixture around over the heat for 1–2 minutes or until the bok choy has become slightly limp. Finally, season with salt and a little black pepper and stir in the chopped flat leaf parsley.

Turn the mixture into a heated serving dish. Sprinkle the mixture with a little soy sauce and serve at once while it is still hot.
TO SERVE Serve this with a soft-textured or creamy dish, such as a savoury custard or gratin.
Serves 4

SALADS

I once wrote a whole book on salads. I worked on it for several months and it was not until the depths of a cold winter that my family protested that they were rather tired of eating salads every day. And a fridgeful of limp, half-eaten salads became a bit depressing. So then I devised some more substantial salads using cooked or semi-cooked vegetables, and their interest revived. As in almost all dishes, the contrast of textures in a salad is one of the keys to its appeal. By using cooked vegetables too, you can exploit those mellow flavors which are absent before heat brings them out. Another effect which works well is to mix hot or warm ingredients with cold. Salads are aesthetically pleasing and of great nutritional value. On a hot summer's day, I enjoy few meals more than a collection of different salads, carefully balanced. Several of the salads in this chapter can be combined to make a summer meal, or alternatively are ideal to serve as a starter for a more formal occasion. Some will make a light meal on their own, perfect for a quick lunch with a friend. One of the best things about salads is that you can actually feel that they are good for you; they have a refreshing effect on the stomach and hardly ever make you too full or sleepy. When my daughter lived in Russia for a year, she sometimes had nothing fresh and green to eat for weeks. We are very lucky indeed to have such a wealth of ingredients easily available, which enable us to create salads for all seasons that are endlessly interesting.

PEACH, ARUGULA AND MIXED LEAF SALAD WITH ROSE PETALS AND ROSE WATER DRESSING

This is the epitome of a pretty, romantic salad. Rose water is available from Middle Eastern or gourmet food stores.

4 firm yellow-fleshed peaches
4 tablespoons lemon juice
Generous handful arugula leaves
3 handfuls mixed salad leaves
1 teaspoon pink peppercorns
Petals of 2 pink roses
FOR THE DRESSING:
2 tablespoons lime juice
3 tablespoons rose water
4 tablespoons grapeseed or
   sunflower oil
3 pinches chili powder
Sea salt and black pepper

◄ *Peach, arugula and mixed leaf salad with rose petals and rose water dressing*

If the peaches are unblemished, they need not be peeled, unless you would prefer it. If they do require peeling, put the peaches into a bowl, pour enough boiling water over them to cover them completely, and leave them for one or two minutes; then drain away the water and peel the peaches. Slice them finely in half-moon slices and then put them back into the empty bowl, together with the lemon juice. Stir lightly with a wooden spoon to coat the slices with the lemon juice.

Arrange the arugula leaves and a selection of pretty, varied salad leaves on a shallow serving dish or on six individual plates. Gently mix in the lemon-juice-coated peach slices. Crush the pink peppercorns roughly in a pestle and mortar, or by pressing down on them in a bowl with the back of a large metal spoon. Sprinkle them over the salad. Finally, scatter the rose petals over the top of the salad.

Just before you serve the salad, put the lime juice, rose water, grapeseed or sunflower oil, chili powder and sea salt and black pepper into a clean preserving jar, seal and shake up vigorously. Taste the dressing for seasoning and adjust it to suit your individual taste.

Pour the dressing gently over the salad and serve.
TO SERVE You can serve this as a light first course or as an accompaniment to chicken or fish. Or it would make a beautiful centerpiece salad for a summer party.
Serves 6

SCALLOP SALAD WITH BROILED YELLOW PEPPER AND MIXED FRESH HERBS

This is a warm and cold salad which can form the main course of a light summer lunch or dinner because the lightly steamed scallops are both rich and satisfying.

1 large yellow bell pepper
1 small crisp lettuce
12 ounces tomatoes
5 tablespoons extra virgin olive oil
1 small garlic clove, finely chopped
2 tablespoons wine vinegar
1 tablespoon each fresh chopped fennel, dill or tarragon, or a mixture of all 3
1 pound bay scallops or 6–8 large scallops
½ tablespoon fresh mint leaves, roughly chopped
FOR THE VINAIGRETTE DRESSING:
4 tablespoons extra virgin olive oil
1 tablespoon wine vinegar
Salt and black pepper

First cut the pepper in half, discard the seeds and stem and put the two halves, skin side up, under a very hot broiler. Leave them under the broiler until the skins are really blackened in patches, then put them into a plastic or paper bag and leave on one side until they are cool enough to handle.

Meanwhile, arrange the lettuce leaves on a large round shallow serving dish. Cut the tomatoes across in rounds and arrange the slices on top of the lettuce leaves. Then take the pepper halves out of the plastic bag and peel off the skin. Cut the flesh up into long strips and arrange the strips on top of the tomatoes and lettuce.

To make the vinaigrette dressing, place the oil and vinegar together in a clean preserving jar. Season to taste, and then shake the jar vigorously.

Pour the five tablespoons of olive oil into a large saucepan or sauté pan and heat gently. Then add the chopped garlic and stir over the heat for 30 seconds. Add the vinegar and season with salt and black pepper; then stir in the fennel, dill and tarragon and remove the pan from the heat.

Bring a little water to the boil in the bottom of a steamer, put the scallops in the top of the steamer and steam for about two minutes only, or just until they turn opaque and become slightly firmer. Do not overcook them, as they will become tough and rubbery.

Add the scallops to the warmed herb dressing in the saucepan and mix gently with a wooden spoon. Shortly before eating, shake the vinaigrette dressing up again and spoon it over the salad. Lastly, transfer the scallops and their juices to the center of the salad, sprinkle with the roughly chopped mint and serve immediately.
Serves 4

DELICATELY SPICED POTATO AND SHRIMP SALAD WITH SOUR CREAM AND FRESH DILL

Fresh dill is a wonderful complement to both potato and shrimp. All three flavors blend together perfectly in this quickly made salad for a delicious light meal. Allow enough time for the potatoes to cool down when you make this salad, but do not chill the salad: it is best eaten at room temperature.

1¼ pounds small waxy new potatoes
3 tablespoons extra virgin olive oil
2 large garlic cloves, very finely chopped
2 teaspoons ground coriander
1 teaspoon ground cardamom
10 ounces large shelled shrimp
1 cup sour cream
Generous handful fresh dill, finely chopped
3–5 pinches chili powder
Salt
Fresh dill, to garnish

◄ *Scallop salad with broiled yellow pepper and mixed fresh herbs*

Scrub the potatoes well but don't peel them. Cut the potatoes in half, or quarters if necessary. Then steam or boil the potatoes until they are just cooked.

Meanwhile, put the olive oil into a small skillet over a low heat. Add the chopped garlic and the ground coriander and cardamom and stir for about four minutes. Remove the pan from the heat. When the potatoes are cooked, drain and put them into a mixing bowl with the shelled shrimp. Pour the oil, garlic and spices from the skillet into the hot potato and shrimp mixture. Mix together with a wooden spoon and leave until cool.

Put the sour cream into a bowl. Mix in the chopped dill and add chili powder and salt to taste. Now pour this dressing on to the cooled potatoes and shrimp. Mix in the dressing gently and spoon the salad on to a serving dish. Garnish the edge of the dish with a few sprigs of fresh dill.

TO SERVE Accompany by a generous salad of mixed red and green leaves and fresh salad herbs.
Serves 4

▲ *Delicately spiced potato and shrimp salad with sour cream and fresh dill*

SPICED CHICKEN LIVER SALAD
WITH FRESH MINT AND PINE NUTS

Warm salads are perfect for a quick-to-prepare, light meal. This dish has a somewhat Middle Eastern character to it. The combination of textures with the warm, spicy chicken livers and the crisp salad leaves is truly delicious.

3 tablespoons grapeseed oil or
  peanut oil
3 tablespoons walnut oil or hazelnut
  oil
2 teaspoons ground paprika
2 teaspoons ground cinnamon
1 rounded teaspoon cumin seeds
1 rounded teaspoon superfine sugar
3–4 pinches chili powder
1 pound chicken livers
1 small frisée lettuce
Generous handful fresh mint leaves
¼ cup pine nuts
1 large garlic clove, finely chopped
2 tablespoons sherry vinegar
1 tablespoon soy sauce
Salt

Put the oils into a mixing bowl and stir in the ground paprika and cinnamon, the cumin seeds, the sugar and the chili powder. Then add the chicken livers and stir them around with a wooden spoon to coat them thoroughly with the oil and spice mixture.

Separate the frisée leaves. Wash them under cold water and dry them fairly thoroughly using a salad spinner or by gently patting them dry with paper towels or a clean linen towel.

Place the frisée leaves in a large salad bowl. Add the fresh mint leaves and mix up the salad well to ensure that the mint is thoroughly distributed. Place a large sauté pan (or, if you have one, you can use a wok) over a medium heat, add the pine nuts and stir them around in the dry sauté pan until they begin to turn a golden brown color. Then add the chicken liver mixture, together with all its oil and spices, and stir for only 5–6 minutes –

this should be just long enough to cook the chicken livers while still keeping them slightly pink inside. Add the chopped garlic and continue to stir for another 30 seconds. Finally, add the sherry vinegar, the soy sauce and a sprinkling of salt. Stir the contents of the pan again just to mix, then remove the pan from the heat.

Spoon the chicken livers on top of the frisée and mint salad, then pour the oil and juices from the pan all over the leaves and serve the salad at once while the chicken livers are still warm but the leaves are still crisp.
TO SERVE Good bread is a natural partner to any dish which leaves wonderful, spicy oils on the plate. An open-textured white bread such as Italian ciabatta is ideal. In any event, this works very well as one of several salads to make up a meal, but it also makes an excellent starter.
Serves 4

JERUSALEM ARTICHOKE AND AVOCADO SALAD
WITH VINAIGRETTE DRESSING

The two nutty, subtle flavors of the jerusalem artichoke and avocado complement each other well to make this simple first course, as do their different textures. The salad is enlivened by green peppercorns, and dressed with a simple vinaigrette dressing of extra virgin olive oil and wine vinegar.

4 tablespoons lemon juice plus a
  little extra
1 pound jerusalem artichokes
2 avocados
1 teaspoon bottled green
  peppercorns
Generous handful parsley, finely
  chopped
FOR THE VINAIGRETTE DRESSING:
4 tablespoons extra virgin olive oil
1 tablespoon wine vinegar
Salt and pepper

◀ *Spiced chicken liver salad with fresh mint
and pine nuts*

Put the four tablespoons lemon juice into a small saucepan of salted water. Scrub the artichokes thoroughly but don't peel them. Then cut the artichokes across in very thin slices and drop them into the saucepan of water. Bring the water to the boil and allow it to bubble for only 3–4 minutes or until the artichokes are lightly cooked but still crunchy. Drain the artichokes and arrange them on the serving plate.

Cut the avocados in half, remove the pit, then carefully peel off the skin. Slice the flesh thinly across in half circles, sprinkling the slices with lemon juice as you do so. Arrange the avocado slices on top of the jerusalem artichoke slices. Scatter the green peppercorns over the top. Prepare the vinaigrette dressing by putting all the ingredients into a sealed jar and shaking well to combine. Just before serving, spoon the vinaigrette dressing

evenly all over the artichoke and avocado slices. Sprinkle the dish with chopped parsley. Serve immediately.
Serves 4

▲ *Jerusalem artichoke and avocado salad
with vinaigrette dressing*

POACHED QUAILS' EGGS WITH SPINACH AND PINE NUTS

If you cannot get quails' eggs, use four hens' eggs and poach till the white is opaque, but the yolk still runny.

¼ cup pine nuts
Dash white wine vinegar
12 quails' eggs
2½ pounds fresh spinach, trimmed
¾ stick butter
¼–½ whole nutmeg, grated
1 radicchio
1 tablespoon balsamic vinegar
3–4 tablespoons olive oil
Salt and black pepper

Put a small, dry skillet over a high heat. Tip in the pine nuts and stir for 1–2 minutes, until they are just toasted. Leave to one side on a plate. Put some water in a wide shallow saucepan and add the white wine vinegar. Bring the water up to a fierce boil and carefully break in the eggs so as not to break the yolks. Poach them for less than one minute, just until the white is opaque and the yolk has lost its transparent gloss – the yolk should still be runny inside. Carefully lift out the eggs with a slotted spatula and leave on one side.

Shortly before your meal, cook the spinach in salted water for a few minutes until soft. Drain the spinach and press out as much liquid as possible. Now put the spinach into a food processor with the butter and nutmeg and process to a smooth purée. Season to taste. Arrange the eggs, spinach purée, pine nuts and radicchio leaves on individual plates. Sprinkle the eggs with salt and black pepper. Just before serving, dribble the balsamic vinegar and oil on top.
Serves 4

EGGS WITH TOMATO AND BASIL MAYONNAISE

The sublime combination of tomatoes and basil is the epitome of summer. The fresher the eggs the creamier their whites will be. This is perfect as part of a cold 'al fresco' lunch on a warm day.

8 large very fresh eggs
2 ripe tomatoes
2 egg yolks
1 garlic clove, roughly chopped
1 tablespoon tomato paste
1 cup olive oil
12–15 fresh basil leaves, sliced
Salt
Black pepper
Fresh basil, to garnish

Put the eggs into a saucepan, cover with cold water and bring to the boil. Boil the eggs for six minutes — this should give you semi-hard boiled eggs with the yolks darker and softer in the middle. As soon as they are cooked, cool the eggs under cold running water. Then peel them, halve lengthways and arrange the slices fanning outwards in a shallow round dish.

To make the mayonnaise, put the tomatoes in a bowl and cover them with boiling water. Remove the tomatoes after one minute and peel. Put the peeled tomatoes into a food processor with the egg yolks, the

chopped garlic and the tomato paste. Process the mixture until smooth. Then, with the machine running, add the oil, drop by drop at first, and then in a thin stream until the mixture reaches the right thickness.

Add salt and pepper to taste. Add the sliced basil leaves to the mayonnaise and process briefly to mix. Spoon the mayonnaise over the eggs. Garnish with thinly sliced strips of fresh basil and eat as soon as possible.
TO SERVE Serve with several other cold dishes or warm or cold salads to make a delicious and varied meal.
Serves 4

GREEN SALAD WITH SPRING FLOWERS

Edible flowers add romance and beauty to food. This combination is very striking, with its strong colours.

2–3 small, crisp lettuces
Generous handful edible flowers
*   such as cowslip, primroses or*
*   sweet violets*
2 ounces fresh raspberries
1 tablespoon raspberry vinegar
5 tablespoons hazelnut oil
Salt and black pepper

◄ Poached quails' eggs with spinach and pine nuts; eggs with tomato and basil mayonnaise

Pull the leaves of the lettuces apart, wash, dry and put into a salad bowl. Lightly mix in the edible flowers, together with their leaves if edible.

Press the raspberry flesh and juice through a sieve into a small bowl. Add the raspberry vinegar and hazelnut oil and stir very thoroughly with a fork.

Season to taste with salt and black pepper and dress the salad with the raspberry and hazelnut oil mixture just before serving.
TO SERVE You could serve this as part of a simple summer lunch, or as a spectacular party dish.
Serves 4

▲ Green salad with spring flowers

CHINESE SALAD
WITH BEAN SPROUTS AND CRISPY SPICED GARLIC

For lovers of garlic and crunchiness this salad is irresistible.

2 small, crisp lettuces
1 bunch scallions
8 ounces fresh bean sprouts
8–10 garlic cloves
1-inch piece fresh root ginger
3 tablespoons peanut oil
2 teaspoons Chinese 5-spice powder
FOR THE DRESSING:
2 tablespoons lemon juice
1½ tablespoons soy sauce
1 tablespoon clear honey
2 tablespoons sunflower oil
2 teaspoons sesame oil
3 pinches chili powder

Cut each lettuce into eight pieces lengthways and put the sections into a salad bowl. Cut the scallions across into ¼-inch slices, using as much of the green part as possible. Mix the scallions and the bean sprouts with the lettuce in the bowl.

Chop the garlic cloves finely and thinly slice the fresh root ginger. Put the peanut oil into a skillet over a medium heat. Add the chopped garlic and stir constantly for about two minutes or until it is browned and crisp – watch it carefully so that it doesn't burn. Then add the Chinese 5-spice powder and the sliced ginger. Stir for 30 seconds and remove the pan from the heat. Leave on one side to cool for a few minutes.

To make the dressing, simply put all the ingredients into a preserving jar. Cover the jar and shake thoroughly. Just before you eat, shake the jar again and pour the dressing on to the salad. Pour the sliced garlic and ginger mixture over the top. Toss the salad and serve immediately.

TO SERVE This spicy salad makes the perfect accompaniment to cold roast chicken or poached fish. It should be prepared no more than 20 minutes before you plan to eat to preserve its crunchy freshness.

Serves 4–5

EXOTIC EGG AND CUCUMBER SALAD
WITH COCONUT AND YOGURT SAUCE

Oriental flavors, such as root ginger, cardamom and coconut, combine well with more conventional ingredients to make tasty and original salads. This is a lovely light egg salad, with a subtly flavored spicy sauce. It is especially good when accompanied by hot steamed or boiled new potatoes for an informal lunch.

2 fresh red or green chilies
1-inch piece fresh root ginger,
  roughly chopped
2 garlic cloves, roughly chopped
4–5 green cardamom pods, lightly
  crushed
½ cup milk
½ cup cream of coconut
6 large eggs
½ large cucumber
1 romaine or other crisp lettuce
Handful fresh mint leaves, finely
  chopped
Generous ½ cup Greek yogurt
Generous handful fresh coriander
  leaves
Salt

Cut the chilies open under running water, discard the seeds and stem and chop the flesh up roughly. Put the chili, ginger, garlic and crushed cardamom into a saucepan with the milk and a sprinkling of salt. Bring this to the boil and simmer very gently, stirring now and then, for 10 minutes. Stir in the cream of coconut and remove the pan from the heat. Leave it to stand for about five minutes while the flavors continue to infuse. Strain the warm spiced milk into a bowl and leave until cold.

Meanwhile, put the eggs in a saucepan of cold water and bring to the boil. Bubble the water for one minute; then remove the pan from the heat and leave the eggs to cool in the water.

While the eggs are cooling, peel the cucumber and cut it into small cubes. Separate the lettuce leaves and cut them in half lengthways if they are large. Arrange the leaves in a shallow dish or on individual plates. Scatter the chopped mint over the lettuce leaves.

When the eggs are cold, peel and slice them across. Arrange the egg slices and cubed cucumber in the serving dish.

Stir the yogurt into the strained cooled milk and taste to see if you need extra seasoning.

Chop the coriander leaves roughly, leaving one or two whole sprigs for garnish. Stir the chopped leaves into the mixture.

Spoon the sauce on to the eggs and cucumber and garnish with the reserved whole coriander.

Serves 4

◄ Chinese salad with bean sprouts and crispy spiced garlic

▲ Exotic egg and cucumber salad with coconut and yogurt sauce

ENDIVE, AVOCADO, CHERRY TOMATO AND WALNUT SALAD

This is a simple salad with an unusual but very successful mixture of textures and tastes.

3 endives
1 large avocado
10 ounces cherry tomatoes
½ cup walnut pieces
Lemon juice, to sprinkle
FOR THE DRESSING:
½ cup sour cream
2 tablespoons walnut oil
2 teaspoons superfine sugar
1 bunch fresh chives
Salt
Chili powder, to taste

Cut off the base of the endives and separate the leaves. Arrange the leaves in one large, fairly shallow dish or on individual plates if you prefer.

Cut the avocado in half lengthways, remove the pit and then slice the flesh lengthways. Sprinkle the avocado pieces immediately with lemon juice so that they won't discolor. Arrange the avocado on the endive leaves.

Slice the cherry tomatoes in half, and add them to the endive and avocado. Liberally sprinkle the walnut pieces on to the salad.

To make the creamy dressing, put the sour cream into a bowl and thoroughly stir in the walnut oil and the sugar. Add salt and chili powder to taste.

Hold the bunch of chives in one hand over the bowl containing the dressing mixture and, using scissors, snip off fairly small pieces. Mix the chives thoroughly into the dressing and then spoon the dressing roughly over the salad.

TO SERVE This versatile salad can be served as a first course on its own or as an accompaniment to broiled chicken or fish. The dressing can also be used successfully for other salads.
Serves 4–5

SLICED WATERMELON, RED ONION AND WATERCRESS SALAD

The crisp and slightly sweet flavor of watermelon makes it an ideal vehicle for salad dressings. This is a decorative and refreshing salad.

1½–2 pounds watermelon
2 small red onions
4 tablespoons lemon juice
6 tablespoons extra virgin olive oil
1 bunch watercress leaves
Paprika, to sprinkle
Salt and black pepper

Thinly slice the watermelon in medium-sized pieces, removing any seeds. Remove the peel from the slices. Lay the watermelon slices in a shallow dish or roasting pan lined with paper towels. Slice the onions as thinly as possible into rings. Lay the onion rings on top of the watermelon slices. Cover the pan with plastic wrap and leave for 30 minutes. Put the lemon juice, olive oil and a generous seasoning of salt and black pepper into a preserving jar.

Remove the slices of watermelon and arrange them on individual plates with the onion rings and watercress leaves.

TO SERVE Just before serving, shake the lemon dressing up vigorously in the jar and spoon it over the watermelon slices. Lastly, sprinkle each serving with a very little paprika. This salad goes well with smoked salmon or other cured or cold fish.
Serves 6

SPICY CHICKEN AND FRISÉE SALAD

This quick-to-prepare hot and cold salad has Chinese undertones.

2 skinless chicken breast fillets
1 cinnamon stick
2 tablespoons peanut oil
2 tablespoons walnut oil
2 teaspoons paprika
1 teaspoon allspice
1 rounded teaspoon superfine sugar
3–4 pinches chili powder
1 large frisée lettuce
3 small red onions
1 tablespoon wine vinegar
1 tablespoon soy sauce
Salt

Slice the chicken breasts across very finely. Grind the cinnamon stick very finely in a coffee grinder or with a pestle and mortar. Put the peanut oil and walnut oil, the paprika, the ground cinnamon and the allspice, the sugar and the chili powder into a mixing bowl. Stir thoroughly to mix. Then stir the sliced chicken breasts into this mixture and leave it for a few minutes to absorb the flavors.

Wash and separate the frisée. Slice the red onions thinly and place them, together with the frisée leaves, in a fairly large salad bowl.

Heat a dry skillet or a wok over a medium heat. Add the chicken breast mixture and toss around for only 4–5 minutes, just until the chicken is opaque. Then stir in the vinegar, the soy sauce and a sprinkling of salt. Remove the pan from the heat.

Spoon the chicken mixture into the salad bowl of frisée and onions. Pour the pan juices over the salad and mix lightly. Serve at once.
Serves 4

▶ *Endive, avocado, cherry tomato and walnut salad; sliced watermelon, red onion and watercress salad; spicy chicken and frisée salad*

JAMIE'S CIABATTA BREAD SALAD WITH ORANGES AND RED ONIONS

A friend of mine makes this delicious Italian-style salad which is substantial enough as a light lunch on its own or accompanied by mozzarella cheese. If possible, use bread which is a day or two old as it absorbs the olive oil better. This salad can be made at least an hour in advance.

2 yellow bell peppers
1 red bell pepper
1 cup extra virgin olive oil
  (approximately)
3 large garlic cloves, thinly sliced
3 small oranges
4 very ripe tomatoes
2 small red onions, finely sliced
8–10 fresh basil leaves
¾ ciabatta loaf
Salt and black pepper

Cut the peppers in half lengthways, discard the seeds and stem and slice across the flesh as finely as you can.

Put ½ cup of the olive oil in a large, deep skillet over a low heat. Add the thinly sliced peppers and cook them very gently until they start to soften. Then add the sliced garlic and continue cooking very gently, stirring frequently, until the peppers are really soft. Then remove the pan from the heat and leave on one side.

Peel the oranges, remove the pith and then carefully pull off the thin skin from each of the segments. Put the peeled segments into a mixing bowl.

Put the tomatoes into another bowl and pour over enough boiling water to cover them. Leave the tomatoes in the hot water for one minute, then peel them and slice the flesh. Add the sliced tomatoes to the orange segments in the mixing bowl.

Add the onion slices to the oranges and the tomatoes. Mix the basil leaves in with the tomatoes, oranges and onion slices, either whole or just torn roughly if you prefer.

Cut the ciabatta bread in slices and then across into roughly 1-inch cubes. Put the bread on top of the other ingredients in the bowl and then pour the remaining olive oil over the bread, allowing it to absorb.

Finally, tip in the contents of the skillet and mix all the ingredients together. Season with salt and plenty of black pepper. Turn the salad into a serving bowl to serve.
Serves 4

WILD RICE SALAD WITH CUCUMBER AND FRESH ORANGE

To me, rice salads often seem very dull. But wild rice – which isn't really rice but a type of grass – has nutty-flavored, chewy-textured black grains which make it perfect for eating cold. Adding the dressing while the rice is hot means that the rice absorbs the flavors and moisture of the dressing much more effectively. This is an easy salad for a party as it can be prepared in advance.

8 ounces wild rice
2½ cups water
1 red bell pepper
1 yellow or orange bell pepper
½ large cucumber
1 small orange
1 small garlic clove
1½ tablespoons sherry vinegar
6 tablespoons extra virgin olive oil
1 small red onion, very finely
  chopped
2 handfuls flat leaf parsley
Sea salt
Black pepper

◀ *Jamie's ciabatta bread salad with oranges and red onions*

Put the wild rice into a saucepan with the water and bring it to the boil. Stir, then cover the pan and simmer the rice very gently indeed for 40–45 minutes, or until the rice is soft but still with a slight bite to it. Uncover the saucepan for the last few minutes of cooking.

While the rice is cooking, prepare the vegetables and the vinaigrette dressing. Slice the peppers in half and discard the seeds and stem. Then chop the peppers finely. Put the peppers into a large mixing bowl. Peel the cucumber and slice it very thinly. Peel the orange, and remove the pith and the thin inner skin carefully. Using a very sharp knife, cut the orange flesh into cubes or chunks.

To make the dressing, press the garlic through a crusher into a preserving jar. Add the sherry vinegar and the olive oil and season the mixture well with crushed sea salt and plenty of black pepper.

When the rice is ready, drain it and turn it into the bowl with the chopped peppers. Cover the jar, shake the dressing up vigorously, pour over the rice and mix in. Leave the rice until cold. Then mix in the chunks of fresh orange, the cucumber, the finely chopped onion and the flat leaf parsley.
TO SERVE Turn the rice salad into a pretty serving bowl.
Serves 6

▲ *Wild rice salad with cucumber and fresh orange*

CARROT AND YOGURT SALAD
WITH PINE NUTS AND STEAMED OKRA

This is a simple but pretty salad with interesting textures and Middle Eastern flavors. My impression is that organically grown carrots really do taste better, especially when raw. Make sure the okra are firm and unblemished.

6 ounces fresh okra
4 tablespoons lemon juice
4 tablespoons olive oil
¼ cup pine nuts
1 rounded teaspoon cumin seeds
5 rounded tablespoons Greek yogurt
2 teaspoons ground coriander
Generous handful fresh mint
12 ounces carrots
Salt and black pepper
Sprigs mint, to garnish

Remove just the top stem end off the okra, without piercing the pod, and put the okra in a steamer over boiling water. Cook for two minutes only, just until the okra turn bright green. Put the hot okra in a bowl, stir in the lemon juice and a little of the olive oil. Season with salt and black pepper and leave until cool.

Put the remaining olive oil in a skillet over a medium heat. Add the pine nuts and stir for one or two minutes just until they are browned in patches. Add the cumin seeds and stir for 30 seconds. Remove the pan from the heat and leave to one side.

Put the yogurt into another bowl and stir in the ground coriander. Chop the mint leaves finely and add them to the mixture together with a good seasoning of salt and black pepper. Peel or scrub the carrots and, using a fine paring knife or potato peeler, shave them into thin ribbons.

To assemble the salad, arrange the yogurt mixture, a tangle of carrot ribbons and the cooled okra in a large serving bowl or on individual plates. Spoon the oil, pine nut and cumin seed dressing over the top. Garnish with sprigs of fresh mint.
TO SERVE This salad goes well as a side dish with cold roast or poached chicken but it also makes a substantial main course on its own.
Serves 4

GARBANZO BEAN, FETA CHEESE AND TOMATO SALAD
WITH GREEN CHILI AND LEMON DRESSING

Garbanzo beans, or chick peas, are one of the most popular beans as they have lots of flavor and texture. The time beans take to cook depends on their age (older beans will take longer to cook) so you simply have to test them now and then until they are done. If you prefer, use canned garbanzos for this satisfying salad, which makes a good lunch simply accompanied by bread and perhaps also a lettuce salad. Remember to leave plenty of time beforehand for the soaking of the garbanzos; if you can, leave the beans soaking overnight.

6 ounces dried garbanzo beans
1 fresh green chili
1 small garlic clove
Juice and finely grated zest of
  1 lemon
7 tablespoons extra virgin olive oil
1 pound well-flavored ripe tomatoes
2 small red onions, finely sliced
6–8 ounces feta cheese, cubed
8–10 fresh basil leaves
Sea salt
Black pepper

◀ *Carrot and yogurt salad with pine nuts and steamed okra*

Soak the garbanzo beans for several hours, or overnight, in cold water. Then boil the garbanzo beans in unsalted water for 30–45 minutes or until they are soft. Meanwhile, cut the chili open under running water, discard the seeds and stem and chop up the flesh finely. Put the chili into a preserving jar.

Crush the garlic and add it to the jar. Add the lemon juice and zest and the olive oil, and season well with crushed sea salt and a little black pepper. Put a top on the jar, shake it up thoroughly to mix and leave on one side.

When the garbanzos are cooked, drain and put them into a mixing bowl. Shake up the dressing once more, pour it over the hot garbanzos and mix together well. Leave until the garbanzos are completely cold.

Put the tomatoes into a large bowl and pour boiling water over to cover them. Leave the tomatoes for a moment, then peel them and cut the flesh into smallish pieces.

Add the tomatoes, onion and feta cheese to the cooked garbanzos, then add the basil leaves to the bowl, whole or roughly torn. Mix the ingredients gently but thoroughly together.
TO SERVE Just before you plan to eat, turn the salad into a serving bowl and mix gently to distribute the dressing.
Serves 6

▲ *Garbanzo bean, feta cheese and tomato salad with green chili and lemon dressing*

73

FISH & SHELLFISH

One of the benefits of a childhood spent in various parts of the world was that I experienced a wide variety of different tastes when I was very young. Children will often only eat fish as fish sticks, but fish sticks were not even available in the countries we lived in. Instead, we had fresh fish and shellfish, cooked carefully and with inspiration as my mother was extremely interested in food. It was only later at an English boarding school that I had the first shock of badly cooked fish which has put many people off for life. Many people who call themselves vegetarians actually continue to eat fish. My oldest daughter, whose favorite meal as a young child was roast beef and Yorkshire pudding, suddenly announced that she was a vegetarian at the age of eleven, but luckily she never gave up eating fish. Fish is never a burden to the stomach; it takes well to all kinds of sauces and goes beautifully with most vegetables. Its texture can thrill the senses and its flavor reach the peak of delicacy. I don't think I could live without it.

STUFFED SALMON WITH MEDITERRANEAN SAUCE

Here a whole salmon is stuffed with a delicate smoked haddock mousse, baked, and then served with a lovely olive oil, lemon and wine sauce with tomatoes, shallots and fresh basil.

3–3½-pound salmon, gutted
8-ounce undyed smoked haddock
  fillet
4 tablespoons heavy cream
2 large egg whites
1 rounded teaspoon pink
  peppercorns
2 teaspoons small capers
½ lemon or lime, thinly sliced
FOR THE SAUCE:
8 ounces ripe plum tomatoes
Zest and juice of 1 lemon
¾–1 cup extra virgin olive oil
4 shallots, sliced into fine strips
1 teaspoon superfine sugar
6 tablespoons white wine
10–12 fresh basil leaves, finely
  chopped
Salt and black pepper
Sprigs dill or fennel, to garnish

◀ *Stuffed salmon with Mediterranean sauce*

Wash the salmon and pat it dry with paper towels. Roughly cut up the smoked haddock and put the pieces into a food processor with the cream and egg whites; process until the mixture is as smooth as possible. Turn the mixture into a bowl, season with salt and pepper and stir in the pink peppercorns and the capers. Lay a large sheet of foil on a flat surface and butter it generously. Put the salmon on to the foil and spoon the smoked haddock mixture into the body cavity, using wet hands to pat the outside smooth. Lay the lemon slices over the salmon. Wrap up the fish securely in the foil and lay it carefully on a flat baking tray. Place the fish in the center of a preheated oven, 400°, for 40–45 minutes, then turn off the heat but leave the wrapped fish in the oven for a further 15–20 minutes.

While the fish is cooking, prepare the sauce. Put the tomatoes in a bowl, pour enough boiling water over to cover, and leave them for a minute or two; then peel and cut the tomatoes into small cubes. Coarsely grate the lemon zest, then squeeze out the juice and keep the zest and juice aside. Spoon three tablespoons of the olive oil into a saucepan over a fairly low heat, add the sliced shallots and stir for a few minutes until they turn soft and translucent. Then add the lemon zest and juice, the sugar and the tomatoes, followed by the wine and the remaining olive oil. Season the sauce with salt and plenty of black pepper, bring the mixture just up to boiling point, then cover the pan and simmer very gently for about 10 minutes. Remove the pan from the heat.

When the fish is ready, unwrap it carefully and lever it on to a large heated serving plate with the help of the foil. Garnish the salmon with fresh dill or fennel. Reheat the sauce without allowing it to boil, then remove the sauce from the heat and stir in the chopped basil.
TO SERVE Pour the sauce in a separate bowl to spoon over the fish and vegetables. New potatoes and a lightly steamed vegetable, such as broccoli or cauliflower, are perfect accompaniments.
Serves 6

Stuffed fish fillets with tarragon and pine nut sauce

Almost any fish fillets can be used for this, but I prefer goatfish, sea bream or red snapper. As this dish needs some last-minute attention, it is best served for an informal dinner.

8 ounces fresh asparagus tips
  (2–3 inches long)
¼ stick butter
2 teaspoons ground coriander
4 ounces shiitake mushrooms, thinly
  sliced
6 fillets goatfish, red snapper or sea
  bream (2–2¼ pounds total weight)
½ cup orange juice
Salt and black pepper
FOR THE SAUCE:
  ½ cup pine nuts
  ½ stick butter
  1 rounded tablespoon all-purpose
    flour
  1 cup milk
  1 tablespoon sherry vinegar
  3 egg yolks
  2 tablespoons roughly chopped
    tarragon

Steam or boil the asparagus tips until they are just soft, then put them aside. Melt the butter in a skillet over a medium heat, add the ground coriander and the mushrooms and stir for a few minutes until the mushrooms have softened. Then season the mixture with salt and black pepper and transfer to a plate to cool.

Lay out the fish fillets skin side down. Divide the cooked asparagus into six piles and lay one pile across the center of each fillet. Spoon the cooked mushrooms on top. Bring up the sides of the fillets to enclose the filling in a loose roll and lay the rolls, join side down, in a fairly shallow, rectangular ovenproof dish. Put a generous knob of butter on top of each fillet and pour the orange juice into the dish around them. Cover the dish with foil. Put the dish just above the center of a preheated oven, 375°, for 30–35 minutes; then turn off the oven and leave the door slightly open while you make the sauce.

To make the sauce, put a dry skillet over a high heat, add the pine nuts and toss them around for 1–2 minutes until browned. Put the pan aside. Melt the butter in a heavy-based saucepan over a medium heat. Remove the pan from the heat and stir in the flour until smooth. Gradually stir in the milk and the sherry vinegar. Put the pan back over the heat and bring back to the boil, stirring all the time. Continue stirring until the mixture is thickened. Pour in all the juices from the fish and bring the sauce back to the boil once again, stirring. Now add the egg yolks and stir over the heat for 2–3 minutes without boiling. Finally stir in the tarragon and the toasted pine nuts and season the sauce to taste with salt and black pepper.

TO SERVE Just before serving, pour the tarragon and pine nut sauce over the stuffed fish fillets, either in their serving dish or on individual plates. Serve with new potatoes and spinach.
Serves 6

Salmon and shrimp sausages with parsley and shrimp sauce

These poached 'sausages' can be kept warm for up to 30 minutes or so in the lowest possible oven and the sauce can be made at the same time and gently reheated, stirring continuously.

FOR THE SAUSAGES:
  12 ounces skinned salmon fillet
  4 ounces shelled shrimp
  2 large egg whites
  1 teaspoon cornstarch
  1 teaspoon baking powder
  2 teaspoons pink peppercorns or
    1 teaspoon bottled green
    peppercorns
  Finely grated zest of 1 orange
  Salt and black pepper
FOR THE SAUCE:
  7 ounces flat leaf parsley
  ½ stick butter
  2 teaspoons cornstarch
  1½ cups vegetable stock
  2 large egg yolks
  4 ounces shelled shrimp

To prepare the sausages, put the salmon and shrimp into a food processor with the egg whites, cornstarch and baking powder. Season well with salt and black pepper and process until the mixture is smooth and pasty. Turn the mixture into a bowl and stir in the peppercorns and the orange zest. Using wet hands, mold the mixture into small, fat sausages. Bring a large saucepan of water up to a rolling boil. Simmer the sausages gently for eight minutes. Drain them carefully in a strainer, and put them in one layer in a lightly buttered, shallow ovenproof dish. Cover the dish only lightly with foil so that steam can escape. Keep the dish warm in a very low oven.

Meanwhile, make the sauce. Remove any thick stalks from the parsley and take out a few good leafy sprigs to use as a garnish. Put the parsley into a food processor and process as finely as possible. Melt the

butter gently in a heavy saucepan, remove from the heat and, using a wooden spoon, stir in the cornstarch until smooth. Then stir in the vegetable stock. Put the saucepan back on the heat and bring to the boil, stirring all the time for 2–3 minutes or until the sauce is thickened and smooth. Now add the puréed parsley and stir over the heat for a further two minutes. Reduce the heat to low, add the egg yolks and stir for one minute. Lastly add the shrimp and remove the pan from the heat. Season the sauce to taste with salt and pepper, if necessary.

TO SERVE Pour the sauce over the fish sausages and garnish with the reserved parsley. Serve with baby corn or baby carrots and new potatoes.
Serves 4

▶ Stuffed fish fillets with tarragon and pine nut sauce; salmon and shrimp sausages with parsley and shrimp sauce

SALMON AND CORN PIE

If you can get them, a few strips of Thai lime leaves added to the filling make this very easy salmon pie even more authentic and delicious.

12 ounces skinned salmon fillet
2–3 sticks lemon grass
1 fresh red chili
2-inch piece fresh root ginger, finely chopped
1 cup frozen corn kernels, defrosted and blanched
Finely grated zest of 1 lemon
2 tablespoons cream of coconut
2 tablespoons butter
12 ounces ready-made puff pastry
1 beaten egg yolk plus a little milk, for glazing
Salt

Cut the salmon into ½-inch cubes and put the pieces into a mixing bowl. Trim the lemon grass, removing any tough outer leaf, and slice the stems very finely across. Cut the chili open lengthways under running water, discard the seeds and stems, then cut the flesh across into strips as thinly as you can. Add the chili, lemon grass and ginger to the salmon, then gently mix in the corn, lemon zest and salt to taste. Add the cream of coconut to the salmon mixture. Finally, gently melt the butter and stir this into the salmon mixture.

Divide the pastry into two equal balls. Roll them out into a fairly thin circle on a cool flat surface. Butter a flat baking tray or a 10-inch circular tart pan. Lay one circle of pastry on the baking tray and pile the pie filling on to it, leaving one inch around the edge of the pastry uncovered. Moisten this edge with water and lay the second circle on top. Press the edges firmly to seal and trim off the edges of the pastry. Roll out the trimmings and cut out a few decorations. Moisten these with a little water before placing them on the pie. Pierce two holes in the top of the pastry to allow the steam to escape. Then brush the pie all over with the mixture of egg yolk and milk. Cook the pie in the center of a preheated oven, 425°, for 25–35 minutes or until the pastry is a rich golden brown. Serve immediately.
Serves 4

LIGHT TUNA CAKES WITH TOMATO, PEPPER AND OLIVE OIL SAUCE

These light fish cakes can be made ahead of time and kept warm in a low oven until you are ready to eat.

FOR THE CAKES:
2 cups milk
1 rounded teaspoon dried oregano
1¼ cups cream of wheat
¼ stick butter
¾ cup grated Cheddar cheese
1 large egg, lightly whisked
7-ounce can light meat tuna, drained and mashed
Grated Parmesan, to sprinkle
FOR THE SAUCE:
1 large red bell pepper
12 ounces tomatoes
5 tablespoons extra virgin olive oil
4 tablespoons water
2 large garlic cloves, finely chopped
Salt and black pepper
Basil and parsley, to garnish

Put the milk, oregano and cream of wheat into a saucepan, and season with salt and pepper. Stirring all the time, bring the mixture to the boil, and allow it to bubble for 2–3 minutes until the mixture is very thick. Add the butter

◄ Salmon and corn pie

and grated Cheddar cheese, then turn the mixture into a bowl. Add the egg to this mixture, followed by the tuna. Allow to cool a little, cover and then refrigerate until completely cold.

Meanwhile, for the sauce, halve the bell pepper and discard the seeds and stem. Place the halves skin side upwards under a very hot broiler until the skins are black; then put them into a plastic bag and leave aside. Put the tomatoes into a bowl, and cover them with boiling water. Drain after 1–2 minutes, then peel and chop them. Put the oil and water into a pan, add the tomatoes and garlic and place over a moderate heat allowing the mixture to bubble very gently. Meanwhile, peel the bell peppers, chop them and add to the tomatoes. Continue bubbling gently for 10 minutes. Finally, remove from the heat.

When the rice mixture is really cold, make the cakes. Oil a large shallow dish. Then, with lightly oiled hands, form the mixture into golfball-sized cakes. Place them slightly apart in one layer on the dish, and place under a very hot broiler for a few minutes until golden brown. Then turn them over, sprinkle with Parmesan and place

under the broiler again until brown.
TO SERVE Reheat the sauce and spoon it over the cakes. Garnish with basil and parsley leaves.
Serves 4

▲ *Light tuna cakes with tomato, pepper and olive oil sauce*

Salmon and Lettuce Ring

Pink and green is one of my favorite color combinations, especially when it tastes as good as this simple salmon mousse wrapped up in lettuce leaves. Because of its attractive appearance, this makes a perfect first course or buffet party dish, or you could serve it as the main course for a light but elegant summer lunch.

*1–2 round or romaine lettuces
   (depending on size), separated
   into leaves
1½ pounds salmon
2 tablespoons hot water
4 teaspoons powdered gelatin
2 large eggs, separated
2 tablespoons freshly squeezed
   lemon juice
5 tablespoons heavy cream
2–4 pinches chili powder
Olive oil, for brushing
Salt
Sprigs fennel or dill leaves, to
   garnish*

Generously brush a 4-cup ring-mold with olive oil. Bring a saucepan of salted water to the boil and then plunge in the separated lettuce leaves just until they turn limp. Drain the leaves well in a strainer by pressing down with the back of a wooden spoon to squeeze out the water. Take care not to tear the leaves, as they will be used to wrap the mousse mixture. Put the lettuce aside to cool. Either steam or poach the salmon until lightly cooked, then remove all the skin and bones and put the boneless flesh into a food processor. Put the hot water into a cup or bowl set over a pan of very hot but not boiling water, sprinkle in the gelatin and stir until thoroughly dissolved. Add the dissolved gelatin and the egg yolks to the salmon in the food processor and process to a purée. Add the lemon juice and cream and process the mixture again until very smooth, then season with a little salt and chili powder to taste.

Line the prepared mold with the blanched lettuce leaves, bringing them up the sides so that they hang well over the edge. Now add a pinch of salt to the egg whites in a clean bowl and whisk them until they stand in soft peaks. Using a metal spoon, fold the egg whites gently into the salmon mixture and then turn the mixture into the leaf-lined mold. Bring the lettuce leaves up over the salmon to enclose the filling, laying on extra leaves to fill in any gaps. Put the mousse in the refrigerator and chill well for about two hours until set.

Before serving, turn the ring out by turning it upside down on a serving plate and giving it a good shake. Garnish the mousse with sprigs of fresh herbs such as fennel or dill. *TO SERVE* Use a very sharp knife to cut the ring into thick slices and serve with a bowl of home-made mayonnaise or Greek yogurt.
Serves 6–8

Lightly Poached Monkfish in Creamy Tarragon Sauce

A poached fish with a light but creamy sauce made from the reduced poaching liquid produces a simple but sophisticated dish that would be just right for a light lunch or dinner. With its firm flesh, monkfish is easier to cook than softer fish but this is also a perfect way of cooking for filleted sea bass. Use larger pieces of bass fillet than monkfish, with the skin still on.

*2 pounds filleted monkfish
4 tablespoons lemon juice
1½ cups fish or chicken stock
½ cup white wine
½ cup heavy cream
1 tablespoon chopped fresh
   tarragon
Salt and black pepper
Generous handful fresh tarragon
   leaves, to garnish*

◀ *Salmon and lettuce ring; lightly poached
monkfish in creamy tarragon sauce*

Slice the fish into ¾-inch slices. Place the fish slices in the bottom of a large heavy saucepan. Add the lemon juice and sprinkle the fish with a little salt and black pepper. Leave the fish aside for a moment. Put the fish or chicken stock with the wine into a separate saucepan and bring this mixture to the boil. Then pour it over the fish. Place the fish over the heat and bring up to the boil again. The moment boiling point is reached, cover the pan with a well-fitting top, turn off the heat and leave the residual heat of the stock mixture to cook the fish for about eight minutes, or until the flesh of the fish has turned opaque.

Using a slotted spatula, transfer the fish to a heated shallow serving dish, reserving the poaching liquid in the pan for making the tarragon sauce. Cover the fish with foil and keep it warm on top of the stove while you prepare the sauce.

To make the sauce, bring the reserved poaching liquid up to the boil and boil fiercely, uncovered and without stirring, for about 10 minutes, or until it has reduced to less than a quarter of its original volume and is thickish and syrupy; then stir in the cream and one tablespoon of chopped fresh tarragon leaves. Reduce the heat a little. Bring the sauce back to the boil, and allow it to bubble gently for about three minutes until it has thickened slightly. Pour the sauce over the poached fish in the serving dish, garnish with whole fresh tarragon leaves and serve immediately.
TO SERVE Simple accompaniments are better with creamy sauces; a few boiled new potatoes (without butter) and a green vegetable, such as perfectly fresh snow peas steamed just lightly to preserve their crispness, are perfect accompaniments.
Serves 4

FAR EASTERN FISH STEAKS WITH CHERRY TOMATOES AND BABY CORN

2 fresh red chilies
1 tablespoon sesame seed oil
2 large garlic cloves, very finely chopped
2-inch piece fresh root ginger, finely chopped
4 monkfish, swordfish or cod steaks
6 ounces cherry tomatoes
2 star anise, roughly broken
2 sticks fresh lemon grass, thinly sliced
Grated zest of 1 lemon
2 tablespoons lemon juice
1 cup cream of coconut
8 ounces baby corn
1 small bunch scallions
Salt and black pepper
Chopped fresh coriander, to garnish

Cut the chilies open lengthways under running water, discard the seeds and stems, and cut the flesh across into very thin strips. Heat the sesame oil in a large casserole over a medium heat. Add the garlic and ginger and stir for one minute. Remove the casserole from the heat. Place the fish steaks, the whole cherry tomatoes and the star anise in the casserole and sprinkle with the sliced chili, the lemon grass and the grated lemon zest.

In a small bowl, mix the lemon juice and the cream of coconut together. Add a teaspoon of salt, and pour this mixture into the casserole. Put the casserole over a medium heat until the juices are just bubbling, then cover the dish and place in the center of a preheated oven, 325°, for 40–50 minutes or until the fish is just cooked through.

Meanwhile, steam or boil the baby corn until they are cooked but still firm, with a slight bite to them. Trim the scallions, and chop them across into roughly ½-inch pieces, using as much of the green part as possible.

When the fish has cooked, add the corn and scallions to the casserole, cover again and put the casserole back in the oven for only five minutes. Season the juices if necessary. Just before serving, sprinkle the dish with the chopped coriander.
Serves 4

COD WITH SORREL AND SPINACH PURÉE IN PUFF PASTRY PACKETS

Although it is straightforward to make, this type of dish always looks impressive. Choose the thickest fillets of cod that you can find, or you can use other white fish, salmon fillets or smoked cod or haddock. The individual pastry packets can be made up in advance and kept in the refrigerator. I like to serve the cod with baby carrots or a tomato salad and new potatoes. If you can't get sorrel, use just 1½ pounds spinach and add the juice of a lemon to the purée.

1 pound sorrel leaves
1 pound spinach
¾ stick butter
1½ pounds thick cod fillets, skinned
Finely grated zest of 1 orange
1 pound ready-made puff pastry
1 egg yolk
Salt and black pepper
Sorrel or arugula leaves, to garnish

Plunge the sorrel and spinach into a large saucepan with a little salted boiling water, cover and cook the leaves for a few minutes just until they are soft. Drain very thoroughly in a strainer, pressing out all the liquid you possibly can with the back of a spoon. Then purée the leaves in a food processor, together with the butter and a sprinkling of salt and pepper. Leave the mixture until completely cold.

Cut the fish into six equal pieces. Sprinkle the fish with pepper on both sides and pat all over with the orange zest. Roll out the pastry very thinly and cut out a piece big enough to wrap one piece of fish. Spread some of the cold purée in the middle of this pastry, then lay on a piece of fish and spread more purée on top. Moisten the edges of the pastry with a little water and wrap up the sandwich of purée and fish fairly loosely, lightly pressing the edges together to seal. Repeat this with the other pieces of fish, gathering up the cuttings of pastry and re-rolling them to wrap each piece of fish. Butter a large baking tray and carefully place the packets of fish, join side down, on it. Roll out any pastry trimmings and cut out decorations for the top. Pierce a small hole in the top of each packet to allow steam to escape. Now leave the packets in the refrigerator until you are ready to start cooking.

Mix the egg yolk with two teaspoons of cold water and a very little salt, and brush all over the pastry. Cook the packets in the center of a preheated oven, 400°, for 25–30 minutes until they are golden brown.
TO SERVE Transfer the packets on to individual warmed plates and garnish with a few sorrel or arugula leaves.
Serves 6

◀ *Far Eastern fish steaks with cherry tomatoes and baby corn*

▲ *Cod with sorrel and spinach purée in puff pastry packets*

COD AND ENDIVE PIE

Cod is one of my favorite fish – the large, succulent flakes are exquisite. Another favorite of mine is fish pie, particularly this one, which is light with a cheesy top of thread-like pasta.

1½ pounds thick cod fillet, skinned
6 endives
1 stick butter
Juice of 1 orange
4 ounces egg vermicelli, angels' hair or tagliolini
1½ cups fish stock
Finely grated zest of ½ orange
2 rounded teaspoons fresh tarragon, roughly chopped
3 teaspoons cornstarch
1 tablespoon water
¼ cup all-purpose flour
2 cups milk
½ cup strong Cheddar cheese, grated
2 egg yolks
1 tablespoon grated Parmesan cheese
Salt and black pepper

Slice the cod into thick 1-inch chunks. Cut the ends off the endives and then cut each in half lengthways, or in quarters if very plump. Melt half the butter in a heavy saucepan, and add the endive with any loose outer leaves and the orange juice. Cover the pan and simmer gently for about 20 minutes or until the endive is very soft. Remove the endive with a slotted spoon and place them in a large, shallow, ovenproof dish.

Meanwhile, cook the pasta in boiling salted water for 2–4 minutes, depending on its size, or until the pasta is just soft but still has a bite to it. Drain the pasta in a large strainer, rinse it through with cold water and place it in a bowl. Mix in a little oil to keep the pasta separate and put aside. Add the fish stock to the pan with the butter and orange juice and bring the mixture up to bubbling; then add the fish, cover the pan and simmer very gently for a few minutes or until the cod is opaque but very lightly cooked. Remove the pan from the heat and, using a slotted spoon, remove the pieces of cod and arrange them among the endive. Add the orange zest and tarragon to the fish liquid remaining in the saucepan.

Mix the cornstarch in a cup with the water and, using a wooden spoon, stir it into the fish liquid. Return the saucepan to the heat and bring it to the boil, stirring until thickened, then allow it to bubble, still stirring, for two minutes. Remove the pan from the heat, add salt and pepper to taste and pour the mixture over the endive and cod in the dish. Scatter the drained pasta evenly over the top.

Now melt the remaining butter in a smaller saucepan and stir in the flour with a wooden spoon. Add the milk slowly and bring to the boil, stirring. Allow the sauce to bubble gently, still stirring, for three minutes. Add the grated Cheddar cheese and stir until melted, then remove the pan from the heat and briskly stir in the egg yolks. Season to taste with salt and black pepper, pour the mixture evenly over the pasta and sprinkle with the grated Parmesan. Place the dish under a hot broiler for a few minutes until speckled brown; then place the dish in a very low preheated oven, 250°, until you are ready to serve. The dish will remain fresh and moist for at least 30 minutes. *TO SERVE* This is best served simply with a mixed leaf salad.
Serves 6

SMOKED FISH AND SESAME BALLS WITH TOMATO SAUCE

If possible, buy undyed smoked fish for this delicious light lunch dish as it has a more delicate flavor.

8 ounces skinless smoked cod or haddock
2 small egg whites
5 scallions, finely sliced
1½ cups fresh white breadcrumbs
½ cup cheese, finely grated
3–4 pinches chili powder
2 tablespoons sesame seeds
Peanut oil, for frying
FOR THE SAUCE:
1 cup plain yogurt
3 plum tomatoes
Generous handful flat leaf parsley
1 garlic clove, crushed
Salt
Black pepper

Using a sharp knife, cut up the fish roughly, then place the pieces in a food processor with the egg whites. Process until the mixture turns to a pasty consistency. Spoon this mixture into a separate bowl and mix in the scallions with the breadcrumbs and cheese. Stir the mixture together thoroughly with a wooden spoon and season with the chili powder and a little salt. Using damp hands, roll small quantities of the mixture into walnut-sized balls. Put the sesame seeds into a separate bowl and roll the fish balls in the seeds until they are covered.

To make the sauce, put the yogurt into a bowl. Put the tomatoes in a separate bowl and pour over enough boiling water to cover. Leave the tomatoes for a minute or two, then drain, skin and chop them finely. Chop the parsley finely, reserving a little to garnish, and stir into the yogurt with the chopped tomatoes and garlic. Season the sauce with salt and pepper and spoon it into a serving bowl.

To cook the fish balls, pour peanut oil into the bottom of a large heavy frying pan to a depth of ¼ inch and place over a medium heat. Add the fish balls and fry, turning them gently, until rich brown all over.

Place the fish balls into a serving dish. Garnish the sauce with the remaining parsley and serve it with the warm fish balls.
Serves 4

▶ *Cod and endive pie; smoked fish and sesame balls with tomato sauce*

TROUT POACHED IN SAFFRON WINE AND OLIVE OIL WITH PARSLEY

This simply prepared dish has a lovely, delicate fusion of flavors. It is perfect summer food.

2 teaspoons bottled green
*   peppercorns*
1 teaspoon coriander seeds
Generous pinch saffron strands
1 cup white wine
1 teaspoon superfine sugar
12 ounces firm tomatoes
2 handfuls flat leaf parsley
4 trout, gutted but with the heads
*   left on*
½ cup extra virgin olive oil
4 teaspoons balsamic vinegar
*   (approximately)*
Salt and black pepper
Chopped parsley, to garnish

Roughly crush the green peppercorns and the coriander seeds and put them into a bowl or jug with the saffron strands. Put the wine into a saucepan with the sugar and bring the wine just to the boil, then pour it immediately on to the peppercorn mixture. Leave the mixture to cool, stirring now and then to infuse the flavors.

Meanwhile, put the tomatoes into a bowl. Pour over enough boiling water to cover them, then peel and cut the flesh into ¼-inch cubes. Leave the tomatoes on one side. Chop the parsley as finely as possible in a food processor. Then spoon the parsley into the gutted body cavities of the trout. Lay the trout in a shallow, rectangular ovenproof dish. Spoon the tomatoes all round each fish. When the wine has cooled, add the olive oil to it. Pour the mixture into the dish with the fish and cover the dish with foil. Put the dish in the center of a preheated oven, 400°, for 30–40 minutes, or until the fish have just cooked through to the bone. Uncover the dish for about the last five minutes of cooking to crisp up the skin. Using a wide slotted spatula, very carefully lift out each fish and put them on to individual warmed plates. Season the juices with salt and black pepper to taste, and then spoon both the juices and tomatoes around each fish. Lastly, spoon a little balsamic vinegar on to the top of each fish, garnish with parsley and serve.
Serves 4

THE MAHARAJAH'S MUSSELS

This dish might have been cooked for a maharajah by a memsahib as it is rather Anglo-Indian in character. The rich flavor of both mussels and mushrooms go exceptionally well with traditional Indian spices. This can easily be served at a dinner party as you can prepare it in advance and simply reheat it at the last moment. If you cannot find fresh mussels use ready-cooked ones (but not those preserved in brine) and halve the quantity.

4 pounds fresh mussels
Generous ½ cup freshly squeezed
*   orange juice*
1 small red chili
½ teaspoon whole cardamom pods
1 teaspoon coriander seeds
3 tablespoons butter
½ teaspoon ground turmeric
2 small garlic cloves, finely
*   chopped*
1-inch piece fresh root ginger, finely
*   chopped*
¼ cup all-purpose flour
250g (8oz) sliced mushrooms
Small handful fresh coriander
*   leaves, roughly chopped*

◀ *Trout poached in saffron wine and olive oil with parsley*

Wash the mussels thoroughly. Discard any which do not close when tapped. Put the orange juice into a very large saucepan. Cover the pan, bring the juice to the boil and add the mussels. Cover the pan again and keep it over a high heat, shaking for a few minutes until the mussels have opened. Remove the pan from the heat. Remove the mussels from the pan and put them on one side (shell them if you prefer). Discard any mussels which remain closed. Strain the pan juices through a strainer into a bowl.

Cut the chili open lengthways under running water, discard the seeds and stem and chop finely. Grind the cardamom pods and coriander seeds very finely. Melt the butter in a large casserole over a medium heat. Stir in the ground spices and turmeric. Then add the garlic, ginger and chili and stir for one minute. Remove the pan from the heat and stir in the flour until the mixture is smooth. Stir in a little of the reserved mussel liquid and continue stirring in the remaining liquid slowly. Put the sauce over a high heat and bring the mixture to the boil, stirring all the time until it thickens. Simmer, still stirring, for three minutes. Then add the sliced mushrooms and simmer, stirring, for about five minutes until they are soft. Then add the mussels and simmer for one minute. Lastly, stir in the chopped coriander.
TO SERVE Serve with either plain boiled basmati rice or boiled potatoes and a green vegetable, such as spinach.
Serves 4

▲ *The maharajah's mussels*

THAI-INSPIRED STEW OF SQUID AND SHIITAKE MUSHROOMS

If you are unable to get Thai sour shrimp paste for this stew, use the juice of a second lemon and chili powder to create the hot-and-sour taste.

> 4 plum tomatoes
> 1¼ cups fish or chicken stock
> Juice of 1 lemon
> 1-inch piece fresh root ginger, thinly sliced
> 2 large garlic cloves, thinly sliced
> 2 rounded teaspoons Thai sour shrimp paste
> ½ cup cream of coconut
> 8 ounces shiitake mushrooms, thinly sliced
> 2 pounds small prepared squid
> Generous handful fresh coriander
> Salt

Put the tomatoes into a bowl, pour over enough boiling water to cover and leave them for two minutes; then drain and peel the tomatoes and cut them into small cubes. Pour the fish or chicken stock into a large casserole and add the lemon juice, tomato, and sliced ginger and garlic. Bring the mixture to the boil, stir in the shrimp paste and continue stirring until the paste is dissolved. Cover the casserole dish and simmer the casserole juices gently for 15 minutes.

Stir the cream of coconut into the casserole juices and bring to the boil again. Add the sliced mushrooms, cover the dish and simmer gently again for another 15 minutes. Meanwhile, slice the squid across in rings, keeping the tentacle part whole, and put the pieces aside in the cool.

When the shiitake mushrooms have cooked, remove the casserole from the heat and leave aside.

Just before you plan to eat, reheat the casserole to boiling point and drop in the squid pieces.

Allow the casserole to bubble for one minute, then cover the dish, remove from the heat and leave for 8–10 minutes while the squid cooks through. Add a little salt, if necessary. Just before serving, stir in the chopped coriander leaves.

TO SERVE Serve with either Thai fragrant rice or basmati rice and a mixed leaf salad.

Serves 4

BABY SQUID STUFFED WITH SALMON AND SPINACH

I actually enjoy the process of cleaning squid and it's not as difficult or unpleasant as many people imagine. However, with the tiny ones, which are the most tender of all, it does take time, so it is a bonus nowadays that they can often be bought ready-prepared. In this dish, within the pure white flesh of the squid packets, the bright green spinach, perked up with orange zest and chili, and the pink salmon create a pretty mosaic; the dill-flecked sauce is shiny and translucent.

> 12 ounces fresh spinach
> 8 ounces skinned salmon fillet
> Finely grated zest and juice of 1 small orange (optional)
> 3–4 pinches chili powder
> 1–1¼ pounds ready-prepared baby squid
> Generous ½ cup white wine
> *FOR THE SAUCE:*
> 1 rounded teaspoon arrowroot or cornstarch
> 2 tablespoons water
> 2 teaspoons dill vinegar
> Generous handful fresh dill, chopped
> Salt
> Fresh dill, to garnish

Remove any thick stalks from the spinach. Bring a saucepan of salted water to the boil, add the spinach and boil for 1–2 minutes or until the leaves become limp. Then drain the leaves well, pressing out as much liquid as possible. Chop the spinach fairly roughly and leave to cool. Slice the salmon fillet into small cubes. Mix the grated orange zest, if using, with the spinach and season to taste with the chili powder.

Remove the tentacle part of the prepared squid. Take a small amount of the spinach and stick it down into the squid, pressing it well in with one finger. Then insert a piece of salmon and repeat the same again until the squid is stuffed almost full. Be careful not to overstuff the squid as it may contract when cooked. Lastly, secure the stuffing by pressing the squid's tentacle part on top. Repeat the process with the other squid.

Strain the orange juice, if using, into a wide shallow saucepan or a deep sauté pan with a cover. Add the white wine, place the pan over the heat and bring the wine to simmering point. Carefully place the stuffed squid into the wine mixture, cover the pan and simmer very gently for only 1–2 minutes, or just until the squid flesh has turned an opaque white. Remove the pan from the heat, remove the squid carefully using a slotted spatula (reserving the liquid in the pan) and arrange the squid on a wide serving plate. Cover the squid loosely with foil and keep it warm in a very low oven while you make the sauce.

To make the sauce, mix the arrowroot or cornstarch in a cup with the water and dill vinegar until smooth. Then stir this mixture into the reserved wine liquid in the pan and return to the heat. Bring the mixture up to bubbling, stirring all the time until thickened, then stir in the chopped dill and remove from the heat. If necessary, season the sauce with salt and a pinch or two of chili powder. Pour the warm sauce over the squid just before serving, and garnish with fresh dill.

TO SERVE For a light meal, serve this low-fat but delectable dish with new potatoes and a mixed or tomato salad.

Serves 4

▶ *Thai-inspired stew of squid and shiitake mushrooms; baby squid stuffed with salmon and spinach*

POULTRY

With my predilection for exotic and aromatic ingredients, the range of poultry now available provides me with endless interesting possibilities. Chicken is often thought to be merely a vehicle for other ingredients. In fact, good chicken simply roasted is rarely disappointing, but the versatility of chicken means that chicken dishes need never be boring. It adapts to any number of flavors and virtually all cooking methods so it has to be one of the most reliable family foods around. And nowadays there are several types of chicken to choose from. Free-range chickens, which live outside and eat a varied diet, have always had a real flavor of their own and are now easier to come by, as are succulent corn-fed chickens. For people who are on a low-fat diet, skinless chicken breast fillets cooked with vegetables to give them moisture and interest are a boon. They are also perfect for stir-frying or kebabs, and dishes where the proportion of meat to vegetables is low. When I first tried guinea fowl, I thought it would taste quite gamey, but it is in fact a more delicate bird than chicken and is best with subtle sauces and seasonings. It is usually available in gourmet food stores, but if you cannot find it anywhere, a home-range corn-fed chicken is a reasonable substitute. Another rare but worthwhile bird is Barbary duck. It is less fatty than the ordinary commercially reared duck and has a flavor nearer to wild duck, though with much more flesh and succulence.

CHICKEN BREASTS AND SUN-DRIED TOMATOES WITH TARRAGON AND PAPRIKA SAUCE

The chicken breasts in this quickly made dish are thinly sliced and cooked with paprika and tarragon, both flavors well known to enhance chicken.

*5–6 skinless chicken breast fillets
    about 5 ounces each
8 tablespoons lemon juice
2 rounded teaspoons paprika
1 large garlic clove, crushed
1 tablespoon fresh tarragon
½ stick sweet butter
12–14 sun-dried tomatoes
1 cup heavy cream
Salt
Chili powder
Generous bunch arugula leaves, to
    garnish*

◀ *Chicken breasts and sun-dried tomatoes
with tarragon and paprika sauce*

Slice the chicken breast fillets thinly across and place them in a bowl with the lemon juice, paprika and garlic. Chop the tarragon and add to the bowl. Stir the breast slices to coat them evenly with the mixture, then cover and leave to absorb the flavors at room temperature for 30 minutes.

Melt the butter in a large, deep, heavy-based skillet over a fairly low heat. Add the chicken mixture and cook gently, stirring now and then, for 8–10 minutes. Meanwhile, slice each sun-dried tomato into 3–4 pieces – if you can get the ones in jars of oil, they are nice and soft.

Then, using a slotted spatula, transfer the chicken slices to a plate. Bubble the pan juices up fiercely for two minutes to reduce them slightly, remove the pan from the heat and stir in the heavy cream. Bring the mixture back to the boil and boil, stirring, for about 2–3 minutes or until it has thickened slightly. Season to taste with salt and chili powder, and then return the cooked chicken breasts to the sauce in the pan, together with the sun-dried tomatoes. Stir the chicken over the heat for another minute, then spoon the chicken and sauce into a shallow serving dish and cover loosely with foil. If you are not ready to eat, the chicken may be kept warm for up to an hour without spoiling in the lowest possible oven.

TO SERVE Just before serving, strew the dish with arugula leaves. This dish goes particularly well with new potatoes and a green vegetable, or with egg noodles or tagliatelle.
Serves 6

PUMPKIN STUFFED WITH SPICED TURKEY AND CASHEW NUTS

If you want to make an impressive centerpiece for a Halloween dinner, this is an ideal dish.

12 ounces skinless turkey breast
   fillets
4 tablespoons olive oil
¼ stick butter
1 large onion, finely chopped
1 teaspoon ground mace
1 teaspoon paprika
1 teaspoon dill seeds
3 large garlic cloves, finely chopped
1–2-inch piece fresh root ginger,
   finely chopped
1 cup unroasted cashew nuts
8 ounces turkey or chicken livers
6–8 sage leaves, thinly sliced
3½ pound pumpkin or squash
Sea salt
Black pepper

Cut the turkey breasts into small pieces. Put two tablespoons of the olive oil and all the butter in a large sauté pan over a medium heat. Add the onion to the sauté pan and stir until soft; then stir in the mace, the paprika and dill seeds, followed by the finely chopped garlic and ginger. Add the turkey pieces and stir until the meat is opaque. Turn this mixture into a bowl.

Add one tablespoon of olive oil to the pan. Add the unroasted cashew nuts and stir them briskly over quite a high heat until they have turned brown, then add the nuts to the spiced turkey mixture in the bowl. Finally, slice the turkey livers. Add the remaining oil to the sauté pan and sauté the livers briefly. Turn the livers and the sage leaves to the turkey mixture in the bowl. Season the mixture generously with sea salt and black pepper.

Now cut the top off the pumpkin. Scrape out all the seeds and strands with a metal spoon. Pack the stuffing mixture into the cavity. Replace the top and wrap the pumpkin in foil. Bake in a roasting pan in a preheated oven, 350°, for two hours or until the flesh feels soft when you insert a small long knife. Unwrap the foil and carefully put the pumpkin on to a serving plate. *TO SERVE* If you have used a pumpkin or a round squash which stands upright, take off the top and scoop out both pumpkin flesh and filling together on to individual plates. If you have used a long squash, cut it across in thick slices. Accompany with some buttered noodles and a simple green salad.
Serves 4

TURKEY AND CUCUMBER STRIPS IN SCALLION AND ANCHOVY SAUCE

A quick, low-fat dinner: the turkey and cucumber are poached in a stock with Chinese aromatics, which then forms the base of the scallion and anchovy sauce.

2-ounce can anchovies
1 chicken bouillon cube
3 cups hot water
2 large garlic cloves, roughly
   chopped
2-inch piece fresh root ginger,
   roughly chopped
2–3-inch stick cinnamon, broken in
   half
2 star anise
1 small cucumber, peeled, halved
   and sliced thinly lengthways
1 pound skinless turkey breast
   fillets, thinly sliced
1 tablespoon cornstarch
1 tablespoon soy sauce
   (approximately)
2–4 pinches chili powder
1 bunch scallions, sliced across in
   ½-inch pieces

◀ *Pumpkin stuffed with spiced turkey and cashew nuts*

Empty the anchovies and their oil into a heatproof bowl set over a pan of gently simmering water. Stir constantly for a few minutes until the anchovies have dissolved. Remove from the heat.

Put the bouillon cube and hot water into a large saucepan. Place the garlic, ginger, cinnamon and star anise on a piece of muslin and tie up the top securely to form a little bag. Add the bag to the stock in the pan and stir gently until the bouillon cube has dissolved. Bring to the boil and simmer for about five minutes. Add the cucumber and simmer for three minutes. Lift out the cucumber with a slotted spoon and pat dry with paper towels. Put the cucumber on to a large warmed serving dish. Bring the stock to the boil again, add the turkey slices and simmer very gently for a further 3–5 minutes, just until they turn opaque. Add them to the cucumber.

Dissolve the cornstarch in a little water in a cup and stir into the stock. Bring the stock to the boil and bubble, stirring, for three minutes. Then add the reserved anchovy mixture and soy sauce. Add 2–4 pinches of chili

powder to taste. Remove the bag and strain the sauce into a clean pan. Bring the sauce just up to the boil again, stir in the scallions for 30 seconds and then pour the sauce over the turkey and cucumber and serve at once.
Serves 4

▲ *Turkey and cucumber strips in scallion and anchovy sauce*

Vietnamese chicken noodle hotpot with fresh leaves

I developed this to remind myself of some of the wonderful hotpots and soups I had while traveling in Vietnam.

4 ounces thin wheat noodles
2 fresh red chilies
3 chicken breasts
3 cups chicken stock
1 cup cream of coconut
4 tablespoons lemon juice
Mixture of salad leaves, including
  plenty of fresh mint
2 tablespoons peanut oil
2-inch piece fresh root ginger, finely
  chopped
3 large garlic cloves, finely chopped
3–4 Thai lime leaves (optional)
8 ounces bean sprouts
4 ounces shelled shrimp
Generous handful coriander leaves,
  roughly chopped
Salt

Boil the noodles in salted water until they are just soft. Drain the noodles through a strainer, then run through with cold water to halt the cooking process. Leave the cooked noodles on one side while you prepare the other ingredients.

Cut the chilies in half under running water, discard the seeds and stem and cut very finely into strips. Remove any skin or bone from the chicken breasts, then slice them across fairly thinly. In a jug or bowl, mix together the chicken stock and the cream of coconut. Then add the lemon juice.

Before cooking, mix up the salad leaves and mint and put them into a serving bowl or into four individual bowls. Heat the peanut oil over a medium heat in a wok or large saucepan, add the chopped ginger and garlic and the sliced chicken and stir for about two minutes. Then finely chop the Thai lime leaves (if you have been able to get them), and add them together with the sliced chilies and the bean sprouts. Stir for 1–2 minutes until the bean sprouts are limp. Now pour in the chicken stock and cream of coconut mixture and finally stir in the cooked noodles. Bring the mixture up to bubbling, remove the pan from the heat and add the shelled shrimp. Taste and add salt if you think it necessary. Finally, add the roughly chopped coriander leaves to the hotpot.

TO SERVE Transfer to a heated soup tureen. Following the wonderfully refreshing Vietnamese custom, place the large bowl of fresh leaves, including plenty of mint, on the table, for guests to throw handfuls of the leaves into their food as it is served.

Serves 4

Quails with tomato, anchovy and fresh mint sauce

These tiny birds are best cooked slowly so the flesh is easy to cut from the bone.

1½ pounds ripe tomatoes
2 small garlic cloves, finely chopped
½ tablespoon tomato paste
2½ tablespoons fresh orange juice
¼ stick butter
8 bay leaves
8 quails
2-ounce can anchovies
1 cup heavy cream
Handful fresh mint leaves, finely
  chopped
Olive oil, for brushing
Salt and black pepper

In a bowl, cover the tomatoes with boiling water for 2–3 minutes; then drain and peel them and chop the flesh very finely. Put the chopped tomatoes and garlic into a bowl, add the tomato paste, orange juice, and a sprinkling of salt and black pepper and mix thoroughly. Spread half the butter over the base of a large roasting pan, then spread the tomato mixture evenly in the pan. Put a bay leaf into the body cavity of each quail and arrange the birds closely together on top of the tomato mixture. Brush the breast of each quail with olive oil and sprinkle with a little salt. Spread a piece of foil with the remaining butter, cover the birds tightly and cook in the center of a preheated oven, 325°, for 1¼ hours. Remove the foil and put the pan back in the oven for 30 minutes. Meanwhile, place the anchovies and their oil in a small heatproof bowl set over a pan of gently simmering water. Stir over the heat until the anchovies dissolve to a creamy consistency and set aside.

When the quails are ready, use a wide, slotted spatula to transfer them to a large, warm serving dish, tipping any juices from their body cavity back into the pan as you do so. Put the roasting pan over the heat on top of the stove, stir the dissolved anchovy mixture into the tomato mixture and juices and bring up to bubbling point. Then stir in the cream and allow the mixture to bubble, stirring for 3–5 minutes, to thicken it slightly. Stir in the mint and pour the sauce into a sauce jug to serve immediately with the quails.

Serves 4

◄ *Vietnamese chicken noodle hotpot with fresh leaves*

▲ *Quails with tomato, anchovy and fresh mint sauce*

Guinea fowl with last-lick sauce

My son found the anchovy and rosemary sauce in this dish so irresistible that he used his finger to lick up every last speck of it! If guinea fowl are not available, use small cornfed chickens instead.

2½ pounds leeks, sliced
2½ pounds small potatoes, peeled and thinly sliced
2 small branches fresh bay leaves
5–6 tablespoons olive oil
3 tablespoons sherry vinegar
2 guinea fowl
4–5 garlic cloves
1 cup heavy cream
1 cup milk
4-ounce can anchovies
Generous sprig fresh rosemary
6 sun-dried tomatoes
Salt and black pepper

Put the slices of leek on the bottom of a large, deep roasting pan. Arrange the potato slices among the leeks, sprinkle with salt and pepper and lay the bay leaf branches between them in a central layer. Dribble the olive oil and sherry vinegar over the top, then lay the guinea fowl on the potatoes and leeks. Smear the birds with a little more olive oil and sprinkle with salt and pepper. Cover the roasting pan with two layers of foil, folded and pressed around the edges to keep the moisture in.

Put the roasting pan in the center of a preheated oven, 400°, and cook the birds for 1¾ hours, taking the foil off for the last 15 minutes. While the guinea fowl are cooking, put the garlic in a small saucepan with the cream and milk. Stir together, then add the whole anchovies together with the rosemary and a sprinkling of salt and pepper. Put the pan over the heat, bring the mixture just up to the boil, then lower the heat and simmer as gently as possible for 25–35 minutes, stirring often, until the garlic cloves are soft and the mixture is the thickness of a pouring sauce. While the sauce is simmering, slice the sun-dried tomatoes very thinly.

When the sauce has cooked, pour it through a strainer into another saucepan, pressing the soft garlic and anchovies through with a wooden spoon. Stir the mixture together and then keep on one side.

Just before you are ready to eat, reheat the sauce gently, adding the sun-dried tomatoes. Pour the sauce into a serving jug. Remove the guinea fowl from the oven and put them on to a carving board. Take out the leeks and potatoes with a slotted spatula and put them together in a serving bowl. Boil up the juices in the roasting pan over a high heat for 2–3 minutes, or until the juices have reduced quite a bit, then pour them over the vegetables.
TO SERVE Carve into neat slices and serve on individual plates with a little cream sauce poured over, and accompanied by the vegetables.
Serves 6

Sautéed duck breasts on a bed of red bell pepper and spinach

This should be cooked shortly before you eat, so it is better for informal meals.

2 large duck breasts fillets (1¼–1½ pounds total weight)
2 teaspoons coriander seeds
1 teaspoon black peppercorns
2 large garlic cloves, finely chopped
1 rounded teaspoon dried oregano
7 tablespoons olive oil
4 tablespoons lemon juice
3 large red bell peppers
1 large onion, chopped
3 pinches chili powder
2 teaspoons superfine sugar
8 ounces small leaf spinach
2 tablespoons pumpkin seeds (optional)
Generous handful lovage leaves or flat leaf parsley, chopped
Sea salt

◄ *Guinea fowl with last-lick sauce; sautéed duck breasts on a bed of red bell pepper and spinach*

Remove and discard the skin of the duck fillets. Then slice the meat across in ⅛-inch slices and put into a bowl. Put the coriander seeds and black peppercorns into a pestle and mortar and grind them together, but not too finely. Add the ground coriander and peppercorns and the chopped garlic to the sliced duck in the bowl with the oregano, two tablespoons of the olive oil and the lemon juice. Stir thoroughly, cover the bowl and leave aside at room temperature.

Slice the peppers in half, discard the seeds and stem and cut the peppers up roughly into ½-inch pieces. Put four tablespoons of the olive oil into a large, heavy-based sauté pan over a low to medium heat. Add the peppers and onion and cook for 15–20 minutes, stirring now and then until both pepper and onion are really soft. Then add the chili powder and the sugar and a good sprinkling of salt. Stir the mixture well and remove the pan from the heat.

Bring a saucepan of water to the boil, throw in the spinach leaves for just 30 seconds until they are wilted, then drain the leaves well, pressing out any excess liquid with the back of a spoon. Stir the wilted leaves into the pepper mixture and turn the mixture into a warmed, large shallow dish. Put the dish into a very low oven to keep it warm just while you cook the duck.

Put the remaining one tablespoon of olive oil in a wok or wide, heavy skillet or casserole over a high heat. When the oil is smoking, add the marinated duck slices and the pumpkin seeds, if using. Flash-fry the duck for 20–30 seconds until it is cooked but still pink-fleshed. Finally, stir in the lovage leaves or parsley. Spoon the duck on to the pepper mixture, piling it up, and serve at once.
TO SERVE I usually serve this with egg tagliatelle or boiled new potatoes, and string beans.
Serves 4

STEAMED CHICKEN BALLS WITH CORIANDER LEAF MAYONNAISE

These chicken balls and their fragrant mayonnaise are good for a cold meal.

FOR THE CHICKEN BALLS:
  12 ounces skinless chicken breast
    fillets
  1 fresh red chili
  1-inch piece fresh root ginger
  6–8 scallions, finely chopped
  1 cup fresh white breadcrumbs
  Finely grated zest of 1 lemon
  1 large egg white
  Salt
FOR THE MAYONNAISE:
  1 egg, at room temperature
  1 egg yolk
  1 garlic clove, crushed
  2 tablespoons lemon juice
  1 cup extra virgin olive oil
    (approximately)
  Generous handful fresh coriander
  Salt and black pepper

To make the chicken balls, roughly cut up the chicken breast and place the pieces in a food processor. Process the chicken until finely chopped and turn it into a mixing bowl. Cut the chili open under running water, discard the seeds and stem and then cut the flesh across into the thinnest possible strips. Peel and finely chop the ginger. Add the chili, ginger and scallions to the chicken together with the breadcrumbs, lemon zest, egg white and a liberal sprinkling of salt. Using a wooden spoon, stir very thoroughly. Then, using wet hands, roll and form this mixture into small balls about the size of a walnut. Put the balls in a steaming tray over gently boiling water, cover and steam for 8–10 minutes or until they are cooked right through. Leave the balls until they are cold.

To make the mayonnaise, put the egg and egg yolk in a food processor with the crushed garlic and lemon juice. Process together, and while still processing, begin adding the oil in a thin stream, gradually at first. When you have a fairly thick coating consistency, roughly chop the coriander leaves, but reserve several sprigs for garnish. Process the chopped coriander leaves into the mayonnaise until well blended. Season the mayonnaise with salt and black pepper, and turn it into a bowl. Cover it with plastic wrap and put in the refrigerator. Before serving, add the cooked chicken balls to the mayonnaise and, using a wooden spoon, mix together gently to coat the chicken balls thoroughly.

TO SERVE Spoon the mixture on to a pretty serving dish and garnish with the reserved sprigs of coriander leaves.
Serves 4

STUFFED AND ROLLED CHICKEN FILLETS WITH ORANGE AND MUSHROOM SAUCE

If you prefer, you can substitute lemon for orange in this lovely dish. To pound out chicken fillets, space them out on a sheet of oiled waxed paper, place another oiled sheet over the top and pound them with a rolling pin or mallet.

  2 medium endives, finely chopped
  Finely grated zest and juice of
    1 orange
  2-ounce can anchovies
  3 garlic cloves
  1-inch piece fresh root ginger,
    chopped finely
  2–3 pinches chili powder
  4 skinless chicken breast fillets,
    pounded out as thinly as possible
  Superfine sugar, to sprinkle
  2 tablespoons olive oil
  1 cup milk
  2 rounded teaspoons arrowroot or
    cornstarch
  2 ounces mushrooms, thinly sliced
  Generous handful flat leaf parsley,
    roughly chopped

◄ *Steamed chicken balls with coriander leaf mayonnaise*

To make the stuffing, put the chopped endive into a bowl with the orange zest. Drain the oil from the anchovies into the bowl, then finely chop the anchovies and add them to the stuffing mixture. Add the garlic and the ginger, then the chili powder and mix together thoroughly.

Pat the stuffing evenly and firmly all over the pounded chicken fillets. Roll the fillets up gently and place them in an ovenproof gratin dish, join side down. Sprinkle them lightly with superfine sugar and smear them with a little olive oil. Pour the orange juice into the dish around the rolls. Cover the dish with foil and cook the chicken in the center of a preheated oven, 350°, for 40–45 minutes. Remove the rolls carefully on to a serving dish and keep them warm in a low oven, covered.

Strain the juices from the chicken into a saucepan and add the milk. Mix the arrowroot or cornstarch with a very little water and then stir this into the juice mixture. Put the pan over the heat and bring the mixture to the boil, stirring all the time. Allow the mixture to bubble, still stirring, for two minutes until it is thickened and smooth. Add the sliced mushrooms and bubble for another minute. Finally, still stirring, add the chopped parsley. Spoon the sauce over the rolls just before serving.
Serves 4

▲ *Stuffed and rolled chicken fillets with orange and mushroom sauce*

CORN-FED CHICKEN WITH CURRIED FENNEL SAUCE

In this dish the chicken is cooked in a pot with spices, yogurt and fennel.

1 tablespoon peanut oil
¼ stick butter
4 corn-fed chicken joints
  (3½ pounds)
2 large fennel bulbs
3 cardamom pods
2 large garlic cloves
1-inch piece fresh root ginger
1 fresh red chili
1 teaspoon ground coriander
½ teaspoon ground cinnamon
¼ teaspoon ground cloves
1 tablespoon all-purpose flour
½ cup plain yogurt
8 tablespoons lemon juice
1½ tablespoons tomato paste mixed
  into 1 cup water
Generous handful fresh coriander
  leaves, roughly chopped
Salt

Heat the oil and half the butter in a large skillet over a high heat. Add the chicken pieces and brown them all over. Put the chicken into a large casserole. Leave the unwashed skillet aside. Cut off the base and stalks of the fennel, remove any marked outer parts and cut the bulbs into 6–8 pieces each. Put the fennel in the dish around the chicken. Roughly crush the cardamom pods and scatter them in with the fennel. Peel the garlic and the ginger and chop them finely. Cut the chili open lengthways under running water, discard the seeds and stem and then slice the flesh across into the thinnest possible strips.

Put the skillet back over a gentle heat, adding the remaining butter. Add the garlic, ginger, chili and the ground spices, and stir for 30 seconds. Then stir in the flour and continue stirring over the heat for about one minute or until smooth. Add the yogurt, stirring in one direction only to prevent curdling. Add the lemon juice to the tomato paste and water mixture. Then very gradually stir the tomato paste mixture into the fried spices. Stirring all the time, increase the heat and bring the mixture to boiling point. Stir until the sauce thickens, and season it to taste with a little salt. Pour the sauce over the fennel in the casserole dish.

Cover the dish and cook in the center of a preheated oven, 400°, for 1 hour. Reduce the heat to 325°, and cook for a further 30 minutes.
TO SERVE Remove the chicken pieces from the casserole with a slotted spoon and fork and put on to a serving plate. Stir the coriander leaves into the fennel sauce. Serve the sauce in a separate bowl. Serve this dish with basmati rice and a green vegetable such as broccoli.
Serves 4

GLAZED GUINEA FOWL WITH BLUEBERRY AND SHALLOT SAUCE

The blueberry and shallot sauce accompanying these glossy brown birds is dark and shiny with a lovely sweet and sour flavor. If you cannot get guinea fowl, this sauce would be equally good with small corn-fed chickens instead.

2 guinea fowl
5–6 ounces thinly sliced unsmoked
  bacon (optional)
Superfine sugar, to sprinkle
FOR THE SAUCE:
8 ounces shallots, halved
  lengthways
1 small sprig fresh rosemary, finely
  chopped
8 ounces fresh blueberries
1½ cups freshly squeezed orange
  juice
⅓ cup superfine sugar
2 tablespoons sherry vinegar
1 tablespoon water
1 dessertspoon cornstarch
Salt and black pepper

◄ *Corn-fed chicken with curried fennel sauce*

Put the birds into a roasting pan and either brush the breasts with olive oil or lay the strips of bacon (if using) lengthways all over the breasts. Roast in the center of a preheated oven, 350°, for 1½ hours. Then remove the bacon, sprinkle the birds evenly with a little superfine sugar and a little salt and put them back on a high shelf in the oven for 15–20 minutes or until the birds turn a glossy, dark brown. Turn off the heat and leave them in the oven with the door open while you prepare the sauce.

To make the sauce, put the shallots, rosemary and blueberries into a saucepan with the orange juice and the sugar. Bring the mixture to the boil, then simmer gently, uncovered, stirring often, for about 25 minutes or until the shallots and blueberries are completely soft. Remove from the heat. Put the vinegar and the water into a cup. Add the cornstarch, stir until smooth and then stir into the blueberry mixture with a wooden spoon. Put the pan back on the heat and bring to the boil,

stirring until the sauce thickens. Season to taste with salt and black pepper.
TO SERVE Carve the birds and serve with the sauce and a green vegetable.
Serves 6–8

▲ *Glazed guinea fowl with blueberry and shallot sauce*

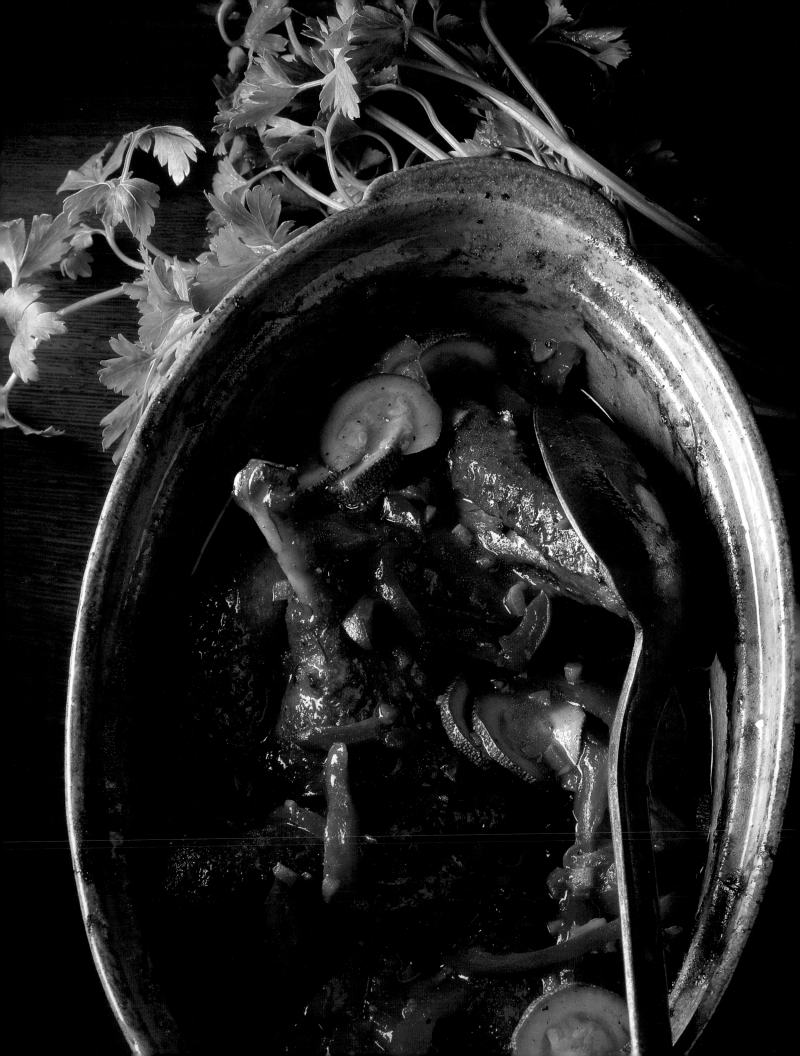

JOINTS OF DUCK WITH SAFFRON, RED BELL PEPPERS AND ZUCCHINI

You can make this glowing casserole ahead of time and keep it warm, adding the zucchini at the last moment.

Generous pinch saffron strands
2 large red bell peppers
¼ stick butter
2 tablespoons olive oil
6 duck joints
3 teaspoons paprika
2-inch piece root ginger, chopped
4 large garlic cloves, chopped
3 tablespoons all-purpose flour
1 cup strained, freshly squeezed
  orange juice
4 tablespoons lemon juice
3–4 pinches chili powder
1 pound zucchini
Salt

Put the saffron strands into a measuring jug and add ½ cup of boiling water. Leave it to infuse. Cut open the peppers, discard the seeds and stem and slice the flesh across very thinly.

Melt the butter with the olive oil in a large casserole over a medium heat. Add the duck joints and fry them on both sides just until the skin has browned and fat is running out. Remove all but a tablespoonful of fat. Then stir in the paprika, followed by the ginger and garlic.

Remove the casserole from the heat and stir in the flour, followed by the sliced peppers, the saffron water and the strained orange and lemon juice. Stir well, and season with salt and chili powder to taste. Then put the casserole back over the heat and bring the mixture to the boil. Stir continually until the juices have thickened.

Finally, cover the casserole and put it in the center of a preheated oven, 325°, for 1–1¼ hours. Cut the zucchini across in half and then slice the halves very thinly lengthways. Bring a saucepan of salted water to the boil, add the zucchini slices and cook for two minutes or until just softened. Drain the zucchini and add them to the casserole dish.
TO SERVE Serve immediately with plain boiled waxy new potatoes and a lettuce salad, which is excellent when the leaves wilt under the hot juices of the duck casserole.
Serves 6

INDIAN SPICED AND FRUITED DUCK BREAST SLICES IN MUSHROOM PURÉE

It is well worth buying the fresh spices whole and grinding them yourself in an electric coffee grinder or a mortar and pestle – their aroma is incomparable. However, this dish is still full of flavor even if you buy your spices ready-ground, and it is an excellent choice for entertaining as it can be prepared well in advance of the meal.

4 duck breast fillets (2¼ pounds
  approximately)
6 cloves
10 cardamom pods
1½ teaspoons coriander seeds
3 blades mace, or 1 teaspoon
  ground mace
1 fresh red or green chili
1 small red bell pepper
8 ounces mushrooms
1-inch piece fresh root ginger, finely
  chopped
3 garlic cloves, finely chopped
½ cup chicken stock
6 ounces seedless grapes
1 pound spinach, roughly chopped
Salt
Coriander leaves, to garnish

◄ *Joints of duck with saffron, red bell peppers and zucchini*

Prick the skin of the duck fillets all over with a fork. Heat a large, dry skillet over a medium heat. Put the duck, skin side down, into the pan and fry just until the skin is golden brown and quite a lot of fat has run out. Using a slotted spatula, transfer the duck from the pan to a chopping board. Reserve the fat in the pan.

Now grind the cloves, cardamom, coriander seeds and mace. Cut the chili open under running water, remove the seeds and stem and slice across very thinly. Halve the pepper lengthways, remove the seeds and stem and slice the flesh across. Purée the mushrooms in a processor. Lastly, cut the duck across in ½-inch slices.

Put two tablespoons of the duck fat in a large casserole over a medium heat. Add the ground spices through a sieve and stir for just 30 seconds. Add the ginger and garlic and stir for another 30 seconds. Add the mushroom purée, the chili and red pepper, stir once and remove from the heat. Stir in the stock and add the sliced duck.

Bring the casserole up to bubbling, cover, and braise the duck gently for about 45 minutes–1 hour or until the duck is tender, adding the grapes ten minutes before the end. Once the duck is cooked, you can remove it from the heat and keep it warm in a very low oven until you are ready to eat.

To finish the cooking, put the casserole back over a fairly high heat on top of the stove. Season to taste with salt, if necessary, and stir in the spinach leaves. Bubble the juices for a couple of minutes to cook the spinach.
TO SERVE Garnish the dish with the coriander and serve with basmati rice.
Serves 6–8

▲ *Indian spiced and fruited duck breast slices in mushroom purée*

EXOTIC CHICKEN PIE

This pie might have been put together by an Anglo-Indian cook during the British Raj in India.

FOR THE PASTRY:
1⅓ cups strong all-purpose flour
¼ cup cream of wheat
½ teaspoon salt
2 teaspoons ground turmeric
1 teaspoon ground coriander
1½ sticks cold butter, cut into small
*   pieces*
2 tablespoons very cold water
*   (approximately)*
FOR THE FILLING:
1 onion, roughly chopped
1 carrot, scraped and chopped
3–4 cardamom pods
½ stick butter
2 teaspoons ground cinnamon
2 rounded teaspoons mustard seeds
4 tablespoons lemon juice
1 cup water
2 fresh red chilies
1 cup ricotta
3 large garlic cloves, chopped
1-inch piece fresh root ginger,
*   chopped*
1¾ pounds skinless chicken breasts,
*   thinly sliced*
6 ounces button mushrooms, thinly
*   sliced*
Sea salt

To make the pastry, put the flour, cream of wheat, salt, turmeric and coriander into a bowl. Mix the ingredients together. Add the butter pieces to the flour mixture and rub the mixture with your finger tips until it resembles rough breadcrumbs. Add just enough of the very cold water, stirring with a knife, until the pastry just begins to stick together. Gather up the dough into a ball. Wrap the dough in plastic wrap and put it to chill in the refrigerator. Then make the filling. Put the chopped onion and carrot into a food processor and process until the mixture is as fine as possible. Remove the cardamom seeds from their pods and grind them with a pestle and mortar. Melt the butter in a casserole dish on top of the stove over a medium heat. Then add the ground cardamom seeds, cinnamon and the mustard seeds and stir for 30 seconds. Next add the puréed onion and carrot, and stir for a few minutes. Then add the lemon juice and water. Cover the casserole and put it over a very gentle heat for about 30 minutes. The sauce should be the consistency of thick cream.

Meanwhile, cut the chilies open lengthways under running water, discard the seeds and stem and slice the flesh across finely. When the onion and carrot mixture is well cooked and mushy, add the ricotta. Stir until the ricotta has melted, then add the prepared garlic, ginger and chili and sliced chicken and mushrooms. Sprinkle the mixture with a little sea salt and stir together. Bring the mixture up to bubbling again on top of the stove. Cover the casserole, lower the heat and simmer the chicken very gently indeed for 30 minutes, stirring occasionally. Then remove the casserole from the heat, and add a little more salt, to taste, if necessary. Spoon the mixture into a pie plate and leave the mixture to cool.

When the filling is quite cold, take the pastry from the refrigerator and roll it out on a floured surface into a size big enough to cover the pie plate. Moisten the edges of the plate and lay the pastry on top. Press the edges down lightly and trim neatly with a knife. Press the trimmings together, roll the remaining pastry out and cut out decorations for the top of the pie. Piece two small holes in the pastry to allow the steam to escape. Cook the pie in the center of a preheated oven, 400°, for 25–30 minutes.
TO SERVE Serve the pie hot with a mixed green salad or a green vegetable.
Serves 6

ROAST CHICKEN WITH ZUCCHINI AND CRANBERRY SAUCE

Cranberries and zucchini are an interesting contrast in this low-fat sauce.

1 lemon
3½–4 pounds fresh chicken
Olive oil, to smear
FOR THE SAUCE:
4 large garlic cloves, chopped
¾ cup chicken stock
1 rounded teaspoon dried oregano
8 ounces zucchini, chopped
1½ pounds cranberries
Handful parsley, chopped
Salt and black pepper

◄ *Exotic chicken pie; roast chicken with zucchini and cranberry sauce*

Squeeze the lemon juice into a saucepan. Put the remaining whole lemon peel in the body cavity of the chicken. Sprinkle the chicken with salt and pepper and smear with a little olive oil. Then roast in the center of a preheated oven, 400°, for 1–1¼ hours.

Meanwhile, prepare the sauce. Add the garlic to the lemon juice in the saucepan. Add the chicken stock to the saucepan with the oregano. Bring to the boil, cover the pan and simmer gently for about 10 minutes until the garlic is soft. Add the zucchini, cover the pan again and simmer for a few minutes until the zucchini are just soft. Then place the contents of the saucepan into a food processor and process until smooth. Put the zucchini purée back in the saucepan and add the cranberries. Cover the pan and simmer again for about five minutes until the cranberries are just soft and beginning to pop out of their skins. Remove the pan from the heat and set aside.

When the chicken is cooked, pour the juices from the body cavity and any in the pan into the sauce into the saucepan, pouring off excess fat if necessary. Put the sauce back on the heat just to reheat and check for seasoning. Lastly, stir in the chopped parsley and serve with the chicken.
Serves 5–6

VEGETABLE MAIN DISHES

This chapter was my greatest challenge. I love cooking vegetables; their variety of color, shape and texture offers constant inspiration. Yet creating a main dish consisting entirely of vegetables, which is sustaining enough without being heavy, is not easy. I am sure many people have memories of shapeless vegetarian dishes, always brown, and either mushy, or with so much fiber that they leave you feeling completely bloated. However, vegetarian food has changed a lot over the last years and a good principal dish can be more exciting than when meat, fish or poultry is the main ingredient. Increasingly, different vegetables are available to us and flavorings are wide-ranging and often subtle or unique. Since I am not a vegetarian myself, I found I had far more ideas if I was cooking for someone who was. Therefore my oldest daughter and a few vegetarian friends have been extremely useful when working on the recipes for this chapter. A vegetarian main dish should not be simply a larger version of an accompanying dish but something which makes as much of an impact as a meat-based dish. You should think of it as the star turn of the meal; it must arrest the attention and remain in the memory both for its appearance and its taste. Many of the dishes in the pasta, rice and legumes chapter also have these qualities.

PEPPERS FILLED WITH GARLIC POTATOES
AND COOKED IN OLIVE OIL

You can make this simple dish with red, yellow or green bell peppers or with a mixture of all three. The combination of the sweetness of the peppers with the garlicky potatoes is quite delicious, and dill seeds seem to have a special affinity with potatoes.

8 large bell peppers
1½ pounds large salad potatoes
6 large garlic cloves, finely chopped
2 teaspoons dill seeds
3 tablespoons plus ½ cup olive oil
Sea salt
Black pepper

◀ *Peppers filled with garlic potatoes and cooked in olive oil.*

Cut just the stem part off the top of the peppers and, using your fingers, remove all the seeds and inner core. Scrub the potatoes and cut them into very small cubes. Put the cubed potatoes in a bowl and stir in the chopped garlic, the dill seeds and the three tablespoons of olive oil. Season the mixture well with sea salt and plenty of black pepper.

Spoon this potato mixture into the hollowed out peppers, pressing the stuffing in firmly. Arrange the filled peppers in a large casserole dish, if necessary placing the open ends against the sides of the dish to help keep the potatoes in the pepper. Pour the remaining olive oil all over the peppers and cover the casserole.

Put the casserole in the center of a preheated oven, 350°, for 1½ hours. Remove the dish from the oven and, using a slotted spatula, carefully lift out the peppers and place them on a large flat, heated serving plate. Place the casserole on top of the stove and bring the pepper juices to the boil. Alternatively, place the juices in a saucepan. Bubble the juices fiercely for 2–5 minutes until they are reduced and thickened. Just before serving, pour the reduced juices over the peppers.
TO SERVE This can be served hot or cold. The pepper juices are delicious soaked up and eaten with crusty bread. A lightly steamed green vegetable is also a good accompaniment.
Serves 4

LEEK AND EGGPLANT CHARLOTTE WITH SUN-DRIED TOMATOES

A golden, crisp bread crust encases a luscious filling of leeks and eggplant.

2 tablespoons wine vinegar
12–14 ounces eggplant
1½ pounds trimmed leeks
1¼ cups olive oil (approximately)
½ teaspoon green peppercorns
8 sun-dried tomatoes
1 large loaf white bread, thinly sliced
Salt
Black pepper

Half-fill a saucepan with salted water, add the wine vinegar and bring to the boil. Cut the eggplant into rounds and then into cubes, adding them to the boiling water immediately as they are cut. Stir the cubes, then cover and boil briskly for two minutes. Drain and pat off excess moisture with paper towels.

Cut the leeks across in ½-inch slices. Put four tablespoons of the olive oil in a large, heavy saucepan over a medium heat. Add the leeks, eggplant cubes and green peppercorns. Stir the mixture, then cover and cook for 10–15 minutes until the leeks are soft. Meanwhile, thinly slice the sun-dried tomatoes.

When the leeks are soft, uncover the pan, and stir for 1–2 minutes until all the liquid is evaporated. Remove the pan from the heat. Stir in the sun-dried tomatoes, and season generously.

Oil a 5-cup charlotte mold or cake pan. Pour the remaining one cup of olive oil into a shallow dish. Cut the crust off a slice of bread and dip the bread into the oil in the dish so that it is thoroughly smeared with oil on both sides. Lay the oiled bread in the bottom of the mold. Line the base with bread slices in this way, and continue up the sides, overlapping the slices and bringing them up over the rim by about one inch. You may need a little more oil to complete this. Then spoon the leek and eggplant mixture into the lined mold, packing it well down. Turn the overlapping edges of the bread in over the top of the filling. Finally place a further slice of oiled bread in the center so that the filling is completely enclosed. Place a metal plate or cake pan on top so that the bread edges won't curl up, but the air must be able to get in around the edges so that the charlotte doesn't steam. Cook in the center of a preheated oven, 375°, for one hour. Turn out on to an ovenproof serving plate. Put the pan or plate back on top and place the charlotte back in the oven for 10–15 minutes until it is golden brown and crisp all over.
Serves 4–5

ROOT VEGETABLE PIE WITH PARSNIP PASTRY

I have a particular fondness for root vegetables; during the winter, I find their sweet flavors very soothing.

FOR THE PASTRY:
12 ounces parsnips, chopped
2½ cups all-purpose flour
2 teaspoons baking powder
1 teaspoon salt
1½ sticks butter, cut into dice
1 egg yolk
FOR THE FILLING:
8 ounces frozen corn
12 ounces small carrots
8 ounces turnips
¾ stick butter
3 onions, sliced in rings
1 teaspoon ground coriander
1 rounded teaspoon caraway seeds
2 teaspoons wholegrain mustard
1 rounded tablespoon all-purpose flour
1 cup apple cider or juice
½ cup sour cream
Salt and black pepper

◀ Leek and eggplant charlotte with sun-dried tomatoes

To make the pastry, boil the parsnips until soft. Mash them thoroughly and leave to cool. Then sift the flour and baking powder into a bowl and add the salt. Rub the butter into the flour with your fingertips until it resembles breadcrumbs. Stir in the cold mashed parsnips until smooth. Wrap in plastic wrap and refrigerate.

Blanch the corn, drain and leave on one side. Slice the carrots and turnips thinly lengthways, boil in salted water until soft, and then drain. Melt the butter in a large heavy pan over a medium heat. Add the onions and stir until soft. Stir in the coriander and the caraway seeds and remove from the heat. Then stir in the mustard and flour until smooth. Gradually stir in the cider and return the pan to the heat. Bring to the boil, stirring, until the mixture thickens. Continue stirring for two minutes, then add the corn and remove from the heat. Stir in the carrots, turnips and cream. Season to taste, turn into a pie plate and leave to cool.

Using a floured rolling pin, roll out the pastry on a lightly floured surface.

Place the pastry on top of the mixture, dampening the pastry edges underneath and pressing down to seal. Trim the excess, re-roll and cut out decorations. Cut two holes in the top to allow the steam to escape. Refrigerate the pie until you are ready to cook. Brush the pastry with the egg yolk and cook in the center of a preheated oven, 400°, for about 25 minutes.
Serves 6–8

▲ Root vegetable pie with parsnip pastry

GREEN BEANS WITH SHIITAKE MUSHROOMS, CHILI AND SCALLIONS

If garlic shoots are available, you can substitute them for the scallions in this Vietnamese-style dish.

*2–3 generous handfuls lambs'
    lettuce or 1 curly lettuce*
2 handfuls bean sprouts
Bunch fresh mint leaves
1¼–1½ pounds green beans
5 ounces scallions
1–2 fresh red chilies
¼ stick butter
2 tablespoons peanut oil
*5 ounces shiitake mushrooms, thinly
    sliced*
Salt

Arrange the lettuce leaves, bean sprouts and mint leaves together in a large shallow serving dish, overlapping the edge. Trim the beans and cut them in half if very long. Slice the scallions across in ¼-inch pieces. Cut the chilies in half under running water, discard the seeds and stem and then slice the flesh across very thinly. Either steam the green beans or boil them in plenty of salted water for only a few minutes until they are soft but still bright green. Unless you are ready to cook the dish at once, run the beans under cold water and put to one side.

Just before you are ready to eat, put the butter and oil into a wok or large skillet over a high heat. When the butter has melted, add the sliced mushrooms and toss them for 3–4 minutes, then add the scallions, beans and chili. Stir for about two minutes or until the scallions have softened but are still bright green. Sprinkle the mushroom mixture with salt, turn it out on to the dish of leaves and serve at once.

TO SERVE As a main dish, serve this with cooked potatoes or noodles tossed in a wok with butter, sesame oil, chopped garlic and fresh coriander.
Serves 6

EGGPLANT CRUMBLE

This versatile dish can also be eaten as a first course or as a side dish.

2 large eggplants
*4 ounces strong Cheddar cheese,
    finely grated*
½ stick butter
2 tablespoons olive oil
2 teaspoons sesame oil
*1½ cups fresh wholegrain
    breadcrumbs*
1 tablespoon chopped fresh dill
Salt and black pepper

Put the whole eggplants under the hottest possible broiler, turning them once or twice, until they are burnt and even cracked outside, and feel soft and collapsed inside. When the eggplants are cool enough to handle, slit them open and, using a metal spoon, scrape out the interior flesh into a strainer. Press out all the liquid using the back of a wooden spoon. Put the drained flesh into a food processor with 3 ounces of the grated cheese and the butter. Process the eggplant mixture to a purée and then, still processing, slowly pour in the olive and sesame oils. Season to taste and turn out the mixture into a shallow, ovenproof dish.

Mix the breadcrumbs with the remaining cheese and spread on top of the purée. Dribble a little olive oil over the top and place on a high shelf in a preheated oven, 325°, for 30–45 minutes or until the top is browned. Before serving, scatter the chopped dill over the top.
Serves 6

BAKED FENNEL AND SHALLOTS WITH WARM SPICY DRESSING

This spicy, aromatic dish is wonderful eaten with bread and cheese for a light lunch or dinner.

5 large fennel bulbs
8 shallots, peeled
1 rounded teaspoon superfine sugar
1 bunch scallions
3 tablespoons olive oil
1 tablespoon sesame oil
*1–2-inch piece fresh root ginger,
    finely chopped*
2 large garlic cloves, finely chopped
2 tablespoons lemon juice
3 pinches chili powder
Salt and black pepper
Fresh sprigs fennel, to garnish

Cut off the base, stalks and any marked outer parts of the fennel. Quarter the four largest bulbs lengthways and arrange them in one layer in a shallow ovenproof dish. Scatter the shallots among the fennel. Season with black pepper and a little salt and sprinkle the top evenly with the sugar. Cover the dish with foil and cook in the center of a preheated oven, 325°, for about 1½ hours until both the fennel and shallots are soft.

While the dish is in the oven, cut the scallions across in ¼-inch pieces, using as much of the green part as possible. Chop the remaining fennel bulb very finely. When the fennel and shallots are cooked, put the olive and sesame oils into a large, deep skillet over a medium heat, add the ginger and garlic and stir for two minutes; then add the scallions and stir for a further minute. Finally, add the chopped fennel and the lemon juice, stir and remove from the heat.

Season the dressing with the chili powder and salt. Spoon the dressing over the baked fennel and garnish with sprigs of fennel to serve.
Serves 4

▶ *Green beans with shiitake mushrooms, chili and scallions; eggplant crumble; baked fennel and shallots with warm spicy dressing*

POTATO AND TOMATO GRATINÉE WITH ANCHOVIES AND YOGURT

This simple dish is a pleasure to make and can be made ahead of time and then kept warm in a low oven. Use plum tomatoes, if available, as they have the best flavor for cooking. If you are totally vegetarian, you can leave out the anchovies but add a little more salt.

> *1½ pounds potatoes, peeled*
> *1¼–1½ pounds tomatoes*
> *2 ounce can anchovies*
> *4 large garlic cloves, thinly sliced*
> *Superfine sugar, to sprinkle*
> *1 rounded tablespoon cornstarch*
> *2 tablespoons milk*
> *1½ cups Greek yogurt*
> *1½–2 ounces Parmesan cheese,*
>   *coarsely grated*
> *Salt and black pepper*

Steam or boil the potatoes until they are cooked but not falling apart. Drain and cool them slightly, then slice them fairly thinly across. Put the tomatoes in a bowl and cover them with boiling water. Drain the tomatoes, peel off the skins and slice them fairly thickly across. Drain and cut the anchovies into small pieces.

Generously butter a large, shallow, rectangular or round ovenproof dish. Put a layer of potato slices on the bottom of the dish, sprinkle them with some of the anchovy and garlic pieces and follow with a layer of tomato slices and a sprinkling of sugar. Continue alternating in this way, ending with a layer of potatoes.

Put the cornstarch in a saucepan, add the milk and stir until smooth. Stir in the yogurt, then place the saucepan over the heat and bring to the boil, stirring in one direction only. Allow the mixture to bubble, still stirring, for 2–3 minutes to stabilize the yogurt so that it doesn't curdle later while in the oven. Finally, season with a little salt and plenty of black pepper and spoon the yogurt evenly all over the vegetables in the dish.

Sprinkle the grated Parmesan cheese over the top of the dish and place towards the top of a preheated oven, 350°, for 45–60 minutes, or until the top of the gratinée is speckled brown all over. Serve the dish immediately while it is still warm.

Serves 6

SWEET YELLOW BELL PEPPERS STUFFED WITH MINTED EGGPLANT PURÉE

Ever since I started traveling in Turkey at the age of 18, I have loved eggplant purées of all kinds. The pale, light filling in this dish, combined with cottage cheese, garlic and mint, enhances the delicate taste of the cucumber. If you want to prepare this dish for a vegan, you can replace the cottage cheese with tahini, which is a smooth nutty purée of sesame seeds. This filling could also be used very successfully in a pita bread filling or as a dip.

> *3 yellow bell peppers*
> *1½ pounds eggplant (approximately)*
> *2 tablespoons lemon juice*
> *8 ounces plain cottage cheese*
> *1 garlic clove, crushed*
> *1 teaspoon superfine sugar*
> *2–3 pinches chili powder*
> *1 rounded tablespoon finely*
>   *chopped fresh mint*
> *Salt*
> To GARNISH:
>   *Small fresh mint leaves*
>   *Chopped mint*
>   *Extra chili powder, to sprinkle*

◄ *Potato and tomato gratinée with anchovies and yogurt*

Cut the pepper in half lengthways and carefully remove the seeds and white pith. Put the pepper halves into a saucepan of boiling salted water and simmer for 10 minutes. Drain and stuff each pepper half with a roughly crumpled ball of foil. Place a large glassful of water in a roasting pan, put the peppers in the pan and cook them in the center of a preheated oven, 350°, for 30–40 minutes, or until soft.

Meanwhile, put the eggplants under a very hot broiler for about 20 minutes, turning once or twice until the skin is charred black all over. As they will be very hot, peel off the skin under cold water, put the flesh into a strainer and press the flesh down firmly with a wooden spoon to squeeze out as much liquid as possible. Put the hot flesh into a food processor, adding the lemon juice, cottage cheese, garlic, sugar, chili powder and a little salt. Process until smooth, then turn the mixture out into a bowl and leave to cool. Stir in the chopped mint.

When the peppers are cooked, take them out of the oven and leave them to cool. Remove the foil. Put the peppers on to individual serving plates and spoon the purée into them. Sprinkle a pinch of chili powder over the top and decorate with chopped and whole fresh mint leaves.

Serves 6

▲ *Sweet yellow bell peppers stuffed with minted eggplant purée*

HOT CHESTNUT AND SPINACH TERRINE WITH RED CHILI

I make this dish as a winter main course. Both chestnuts and spinach are particularly enhanced by fresh ginger, and the slivers of chili give the terrine a lovely bite. Use the left-over egg yolks for a lovely rich cake or for home-made mayonnaise.

1 large plump red chili
1½ pounds spinach, trimmed
2-inch piece fresh root ginger, finely chopped
3–4 garlic cloves, finely chopped
Finely grated zest of 1 orange
1 stick sweet butter
Bunch flat leaf parsley
1 large egg
4 egg whites
12–14 ounces vacuum packed or canned whole chestnuts
Salt

Cut the chili in half under running water and discard the seeds and stem. Cut the chili flesh across into very thin short strips. Bring a little salted water to the boil, add the washed spinach, cover the pan and boil the spinach until the leaves are soft. Drain the spinach well and press out as much liquid as possible with the back of a spoon. To thoroughly dry the spinach, pat the leaves between paper towels. Put the spinach into a food processor and add the ginger and garlic and the orange zest. Sprinkle the mixture quite generously with salt as it will be diluted by the eggs later. Add the butter and process until finely puréed. Leave the mixture to cool for about 10 minutes.

Meanwhile, line the sides of a 4-cup pan or terrine dish with buttered waxed paper. Scatter the chili strips over the base and also up the sides by pressing them against the buttered paper. Then press on several good sprigs of flat leaf parsley. Add the egg and egg whites to the spinach purée in the food processor and process thoroughly. Add extra salt to taste if needed. Leave the mixture to cool completely.

Put a large roasting pan of hot water in the center of the oven and heat the oven to 325°. Add the chestnuts to the purée and mix in gently. Spoon the mixture carefully into the prepared pan or dish so as not to disarrange the strips of chili and parsley. Butter a large piece of foil and place it loosely on top, but pressing the edges to seal. Pierce two or three holes in the foil to allow the steam to escape. Put the pan or dish into the water in the roasting pan and cook the terrine for 1¼–1½ hours or until a small knife inserted in the center comes out clean.

If you are eating immediately, remove it from the heat and leave for a few minutes. Then put the pan or dish upside down against an oblong serving dish, giving it a good shake to turn the terrine out.
TO SERVE Carefully remove the waxed paper and serve warm, with a frisée salad with walnuts and good bread or new potatoes.
Serves 4–6

NEW POTATOES WITH GREEN LENTILS AND SCALLIONS

This is a nutritious dish which you can serve as a main course accompanied by green vegetables or a salad. It can be prepared quickly in advance and then it needs only a minute or two last-minute cooking in a wok. When I first made this, the English countryside was full of wild garlic; the star-like white flowers thrown on to this dish looked very pretty and tasted good too. If garlic shoots are available, try substituting them for the chives.

3 ounces green lentils
1 pound small waxy new potatoes
6–8 scallions
Generous handful chives
4 tablespoons extra virgin olive oil
2 tablespoons balsamic vinegar
Sea salt
Black pepper

Bring a large saucepan of salted water to the boil. Rinse the green lentils thoroughly, then cook them in the boiling water for 15–30 minutes or until tender. Drain the lentils and leave on one side. Meanwhile, either steam or boil the potatoes until they are just soft right through, then drain and cut them in half, unless they are really small. Trim the base from the scallions. Cut the chives and scallions across in strips of about 3 inches, using as much of the green part of the scallion as possible.

Just before serving, put the olive oil in a wok over a high heat, then add the lentils, potatoes, scallions and chives. Toss the mixture over the high heat for a few minutes or until the scallions and chives are bright green and just softened.

Season well with sea salt and plenty of black pepper. Toss the vegetables once more and turn them out into a heated serving dish. Sprinkle the balsamic vinegar over the top.
Serves 3–4

◄ Hot chestnut and spinach terrine with red chili

▲ New potatoes with green lentils and scallions

SPINACH, PARSLEY AND SORREL PURÉE WITH BALSAMIC BRAISED LEEKS

Serve this either as one of several vegetarian dishes for a main course, or make it into a main dish itself by adding thin slivers of skinless chicken breast to the braised leeks when they are cooked. Simply stir the chicken around in the pan with the leeks for a few minutes until all the liquid has evaporated.

1–1½ pounds small thin leeks,
  trimmed
3 tablespoons olive oil
5–6 tablespoons balsamic vinegar
1 pound spinach
Large bunch parsley
Generous handful sorrel leaves
½ stick butter
Finely grated zest of ½ orange
Salt and black pepper

Cut the leeks across into 2-inch pieces, then wash and drain. Put the olive oil into a wide, heavy saucepan or a deep sauté pan over a low heat. Add the leeks, cover the pan and cook very gently until they begin to soften. Then remove the cover, add three tablespoons of the balsamic vinegar and continue cooking the leeks gently in the open pan, stirring now and then, for 20–30 minutes. Add the remaining vinegar at separate intervals until the leeks are very soft and browned, and the balsamic juices have almost evaporated. Season the mixture to taste with salt and plenty of freshly ground black pepper.

While the leeks are cooking, prepare the spinach purée. Either steam or boil the spinach in a little water for a few minutes until just soft, then add the parsley and cook for another minute. Finally, add the sorrel leaves and stir until the leaves go limp and lose their bright green color. Drain the leaves very well, pressing out any excess liquid with the back of a spoon. Put the mixture into a food processor with the butter and grated orange zest. Process until smoothly puréed. Season the purée to taste with salt and black pepper and spoon it out into a wide gratinée or serving dish. Cover loosely with foil and keep the dish warm in a very low oven until the leeks are ready. Arrange the leeks on top of the spinach and serve immediately.
Serves 6

ROOT VEGETABLE MOUSSE WITH HONEYED TOP

The combination of creamy sweet carrots, parsnips and a hint of peppery turnip in this chilled mousse is an unexpected pleasure. Cold mousses are always popular on a summer buffet table, if you are entertaining.

FOR THE MOUSSE:
  8 ounces carrots, roughly chopped
  8 ounces parsnips, roughly chopped
  1 cup heavy cream
  2 eggs
  ¼ whole nutmeg, grated
  Salt
  Chili powder
FOR THE TOPPING:
  3 tablespoons sherry vinegar
  2 rounded tablespoons honey
  5 tablespoons extra virgin olive oil
  1 large garlic clove, finely sliced
  1 large carrot, cut into thin strips
  1 turnip, cut into thin strips
  2–3 sprigs flat leaf parsley, to
    garnish
  Salt
  Black pepper

◄ Spinach, parsley and sorrel purée with balsamic braised leeks

Smear a deep 6-inch cake pan with olive oil and put a piece of oiled waxed paper in the bottom. To make the mousse, boil both the carrots and parsnips in salted water until soft. Drain the vegetables and put them into a food processor. Add the cream and eggs and process the mixture until very smooth. Process in the nutmeg with a little salt and chili powder to taste. Spoon the mixture into the prepared cake pan. Cook the mousse just below the center of a preheated oven, 300°, for 50–60 minutes, or until the mousse is just firm to a light touch in the center. Then remove the mousse from the oven and leave it until cold. Meanwhile, make the topping.

Put the sherry vinegar, honey and olive oil in a saucepan over a medium heat. When the honey has melted, add the sliced garlic, carrot and turnip and stir over the heat for 4–5 minutes. Season the vegetable mixture to taste with salt and black pepper and leave it until cold.

When the mousse is cold, very carefully loosen the sides with a flexible knife. Turn the mousse out, giving it a gentle shake, on to a serving plate. Remove the disc of waxed paper and refrigerate the mousse until you are ready to eat.
TO SERVE Spoon the honeyed vegetable topping on to the mousse and finally garnish with the sprigs of fresh flat leaf parsley.
Serves 4

▲ Root vegetable mousse with honeyed top

TUE'S MOTHER'S VEGETABLE DISH

Tue was my guide on a recent visit to the imperial city of Hue in Vietnam. This vegetable dish, based on one of his mother's favorite recipes, can be adapted by adding slivers of chicken, fish or shellfish.

2 fresh red chilies
1 bunch scallions
2 cups cream of coconut
1 rounded teaspoon salt
1 romaine lettuce
½-inch piece root ginger
3 large garlic cloves
10 ounces cherry tomatoes
6 ounces shiitake mushrooms
4 ounces baby corn
8 ounces canned water chestnuts
Handful fresh mint leaves
Handful fresh coriander leaves
4–5 Thai lime leaves (optional)
2 handfuls small spinach leaves
8 ounces bean sprouts
8 tablespoons lemon juice
2 tablespoons peanut oil

Prepare all the ingredients before you start to cook. Cut the chilies open lengthways under running water, discard the seeds and stem and then slice the flesh across as thinly as possible. Prepare the scallions by trimming the tops and bottoms, and cut them across in ¼-inch pieces, using as much of the green part as possible. Put the cream of coconut into a measuring jug and add the salt. Slice the romaine lettuce across in 1-inch strips. Finely chop the fresh root ginger and the garlic. Halve the cherry tomatoes. Slice the shiitake mushrooms across thinly. Slice the baby corn in half lengthways. Drain and slice the canned water chestnuts thickly. Roughly chop the fresh mint and coriander leaves. Finely chop the Thai lime leaves, if you have been able to get them. Have ready the spinach leaves, the bean sprouts and the lemon juice.

To cook, heat the peanut oil in a wok or a large heavy casserole dish over a high heat. Add the shiitake mushrooms and stir for 1–2 minutes until they begin to soften. Then stir in the chopped ginger and garlic and the Thai lime leaves (if you are using them), followed by the chopped chilies. Immediately add the halved cherry tomatoes, the halved baby corn and the sliced water chestnuts and then pour in the cream of coconut.

Bring the mixture to the boil, bubble in the open pan for no more than two minutes, then add the sliced scallions and the bean sprouts. Next, add the sliced lettuce and spinach leaves and stir in until they are just wilted.

Finally, stir in the lemon juice followed by the chopped mint and coriander leaves, and then serve immediately before the vegetables lose their freshness.
TO SERVE Serve this dish with an accompaniment of Chinese noodles or rice to mop up the milky juices.
Serves 4

HOT STUFFED AVOCADOS WITH MOZZARELLA CHEESE

This light meal of avocados, filled with a scarlet mixture of sweet pepper purée and tomatoes, makes a lovely surprise when served with good crusty bread. Use really large avocados, and plum tomatoes if they are available. This dish will serve eight people if you use it for a first course. If you want a special treat, get the authentic *mozzarella di bufala*, made with buffalo milk.

1 red bell pepper
3 large unpeeled garlic cloves
1 tablespoon lemon juice
2 teaspoons superfine sugar
2 tomatoes
10–12 fresh basil or mint leaves, thinly sliced
4 large ripe avocados
5 ounces fresh mozzarella cheese, thinly sliced
Salt
Black pepper

Cut open the red bell pepper, discard the seeds and stem and cut up the flesh roughly. Put it into a saucepan of boiling water with the unpeeled garlic and simmer for about 10 minutes. Drain and put the pepper and garlic (the garlic skins should have popped off while being boiled) into a food processor, together with most of the lemon juice, reserving just a little for brushing. Season with salt, pepper and sugar. Process to a smooth purée and turn the mixture into a bowl.

Put the tomatoes into a bowl and cover them with boiling water. Leave them for one minute, then peel and chop the flesh into small pieces. Stir the chopped tomatoes and basil or mint into the red purée. Halve and pit the avocados and smear the flesh with lemon juice to prevent discoloration.

Put the avocado halves in a shallow ovenproof dish and fill the hollow with the pepper and tomato mixture. Arrange the slices of mozzarella over the stuffing and around the edges of the avocados. Cook them in the center of a preheated oven, 375°, for 10–15 minutes. Serve immediately.
Serves 4

▲ *Hot stuffed avocados with mozzarella cheese*

◄ *Tue's mother's vegetable dish*

LEEK AND RED ONION COBBLER WITH POTATO AND CHEESE PASTRY

Everyone loves this combination of tastes, and leeks are one of my favorite vegetables. As an alternative to leeks, you can use bulb fennel.

FOR THE FILLING:
  2 pounds leeks
  2 large red onions
  ¼ stick butter
  4 tablespoons extra virgin olive oil
  2 teaspoons caraway seeds
  4–5 pinches chili powder
  Sea salt
FOR THE PASTRY TOP:
  12 ounces potatoes
  1½ cups self-raising flour
  1 rounded teaspoon salt
  3 ounces strong flavoured grated cheese
  1¼ sticks butter
  1 egg yolk
  1 tablespoon grated Parmesan cheese

To make the filling, trim the leeks and cut into 1-inch pieces, using as much of the green part as possible. Peel the onions and chop into roughly 1-inch pieces. Melt the butter with the olive oil in a large, deep skillet. Add the sliced leeks and onions and caraway seeds. Cook over a medium heat, stirring fairly often, until the leeks and onions have softened. Season the mixture to taste with the chili powder and salt. Turn the filling into a large, shallow, ovenproof dish. Leave the filling on one side to cool. Meanwhile, make the pastry.

For the pastry, peel the potatoes. Steam or boil the potatoes until they are soft. Mash them in a bowl until they are as smooth as possible. Leave the mashed potatoes until cold.

Sift together the flour and salt into another bowl. Stir in the grated cheese. Then add the butter, cut into small pieces, and rub with your fingertips until the mixture resembles rough breadcrumbs. Work in the cold mashed potato with your hands and knead the mixture to make a smooth dough. If you are not using the dough immediately, form it into a ball, wrap it in plastic wrap and refrigerate.

When the leek mixture is cold, roll the pastry out to about ¼ inch thick on a floured board. Using a 2½-inch cookie cutter, cut the pastry into circles, re-rolling the scraps. Arrange the circles overlapping on top of the leek mixture. Then refrigerate the dish until you are ready to cook.

To cook, brush the pastry circles with egg yolk and then sprinkle with the Parmesan cheese. Cook the cobbler in the center of a preheated oven, 400°, for 25–30 minutes until the pastry has turned a rich golden brown.
Serves 6

GARDEN PIE

One of the difficulties of making good vegetarian main dishes is how to make them substantial enough without them being rather stodgy. Pies are often a satisfactory solution. This is a lovely fresh-tasting pie which you can decorate to look pretty and inviting. Use plum tomatoes if they are available, as their flavor is much better. Accompany this dish with new potatoes and a salad.

  12 ounces tomatoes
  8 ounces small zucchini
  4 ounces baby corn
  4 ounces frozen small peas
  4 ounces bean sprouts
  1 large garlic clove, finely chopped
  1 sprig fresh tarragon, roughly chopped
  2 egg yolks
  1 cup heavy cream
  13 ounces frozen puff pastry
  Milk, for brushing
  Salt and black pepper

◀ *Leek and red onion cobbler with potato and cheese pastry*

Put the tomatoes into a bowl, cover them with boiling water and leave for one minute. Peel and cut them into small pieces. Slice the zucchini across very finely. Slice the baby corn thinly lengthways. Put the peas into a strainer and pour water over just to defrost them. Put the prepared vegetables, bean sprouts, garlic and tarragon into a buttered, fairly shallow ovenproof dish, so the dish is almost filled. Put the egg yolks into a bowl and lightly whisk in the cream. Season the cream well with salt and pepper and pour it over the vegetables in the dish.

Roll out the pastry into a piece big enough to fit the top of the dish. Moisten the edges of the dish, lay the pastry on top and press gently around the edge to seal. Cut the pastry edges off neatly. Re-roll the scraps of pastry and cut out shapes for decoration. Moisten the underside of the shapes and arrange them on the pie. Cut two small holes in the center of the pie to allow the steam to escape. If there is time, chill the pie in the refrigerator for at least 30 minutes. When ready to cook, brush the pie lightly with a little milk and cook it just above the center of a preheated oven, 400°, for about 30 minutes or until the pastry is puffed and a rich brown.
Serves 4

▲ *Garden pie*

BLANQUETTE OF ENDIVES, TURNIPS AND SHALLOTS WITH HONEY AND MUSTARD

This lovely creamy casserole has a tantalizing fusion of flavors; sweet, peppery and slightly bitter all at once.

6 large endives
¼ stick butter
3 tablespoons olive oil
1 pound baby turnips, trimmed
12 ounces shallots, peeled
8 juniper berries, roughly crushed
2 tablespoons all-purpose flour
1½ cups milk
1 cup heavy cream
1 tablespoon honey
5 teaspoons wholegrain mustard
2 tablespoons lemon juice
2 egg yolks
Generous handful fresh dill, roughly chopped
Salt and black pepper

Cut just the very bottom off the whole endives. Gently melt the butter with the olive oil in a large casserole on top of the stove. Remove the casserole from the heat and add the prepared turnips, shallots and endives. Stir with a wooden spoon to coat the vegetables with the butter and oil. Add the crushed juniper berries. Then stir in the flour thoroughly.

Put the milk and ½ cup of the cream into a saucepan with the honey and mustard. Season the mixture with salt and black pepper. Place the pan over a medium heat, stirring all the time until the honey has dissolved into the milk. Add the heated milk, cream and honey to the vegetables in the casserole and stir. Put the casserole back over a fairly high heat and bring the mixture to the boil, stirring all the time until the liquid thickens. Then cover the casserole and cook in the center of a preheated oven, 325°, for one hour, or until the vegetables are soft.

Remove the casserole from the oven and stir in the lemon juice. Put the remaining heavy cream into a bowl with the egg yolks and whisk lightly together with a fork. Then stir the cream into the casserole. Taste the mixture and add more seasoning or mustard if you like. Before serving, put the casserole back over a medium heat on top of the stove just to reheat, without boiling. Lastly, stir the chopped dill into the casserole.
TO SERVE Serve with new potatoes and a green vegetable.
Serves 6

BEET TART WITH CREAM CHEESE AND CARAWAY PASTRY

For a light lunch or dinner, this scarlet upside-down beet tart looks beautiful when it is accompanied by a green mixed leaf salad. The crumbly, crusty cream cheese pastry is extremely easy and takes only a few minutes to make, and its flavor and texture contrast well with the smooth slices of cooked beet. You can make the tart in advance and reheat it, still in its dish, or, if you prefer, you can cook the tart and keep it warm in a very low oven until you are ready to serve.

½ cup cream cheese
1 stick sweet butter
2 teaspoons caraway seeds
1½ cups all-purpose flour
2 teaspoons baking powder
3 generous pinches chili powder
1¼ pounds (approximately) cooked and peeled small fresh beet, thinly sliced
Salt
Black pepper
Whole sprigs flat leaf parsley, to garnish

◄ *Blanquette of endives, turnips and shallots with honey and mustard*

Put the cream cheese and ¾ stick of the butter into a food processor and process briefly to mix together. Then add the caraway seeds, flour, baking powder, chili powder and a good sprinkling of salt. Process once again to form a dough. Pat the dough into a ball, wrap it in plastic wrap and refrigerate for about 20 minutes.

Smear the bottom of a 9-inch earthenware dish with the remaining butter and sprinkle it evenly with salt and a little black pepper. Lay the beet slices in a neatly overlapping layer on the bottom of the dish. Continue layering in this way with the remaining beet until all the slices are in the dish.

Take the dough out of the refrigerator. Roll out the cold dough on a lightly floured surface into a circle very slightly bigger than the dish. Lay the pastry on top of the beet slices and press the edges down the inner sides of the dish, making a thick rim. Pierce two small holes in the pastry with a skewer to allow the steam to escape. Cook the tart in the center of a preheated oven, 400°, for about 30 minutes or until the pastry is browned. Remove the tart from the oven and leave it to cool for 8–10 minutes. Then turn it out on a serving plate by giving the dish a shake against the plate before carefully lifting it off the tart.
TO SERVE Garnish the top of the tart with a few perfect sprigs of flat leaf parsley and serve the tart warm. If you like, you can serve a bowl of plain yogurt, seasoned with salt and coarsely ground black pepper, as a sauce.
Serves 4

▲ *Beet tart with cream cheese and caraway pastry*

DESSERTS & CAKES

There is no doubt that eating large quantities of desserts and cakes does neither your figure or your teeth much good, but there is also no doubt that the making and eating of desserts and cakes is a therapeutic activity and can make you feel happier. To me, a meal like Sunday lunch without a dessert seems not to be the real thing at all and a sweet surprise at the end of a dinner party certainly makes the most appreciated finale. However, though there is so much scope in this area of cooking, it seems to leave many people at a loss. You do have to balance desserts well with the rest of the meal; a rich and substantial dessert after a heavy main course is clearly a mistake. But a sharp sorbet might be just the thing. Equally after a delicate fish dish, a buttery crusted tart or something chocolaty can be perfect. Cakes are in a way even more of an indulgence than desserts, but a cozy supper with a good cake is often one of the most enjoyable meals. The ingredients for cake-making are a great pleasure to work with and what happens to cakes once put in the oven has never ceased to seem a miracle. And as for the eating; well, I can't remember ever being able to restrict myself to eating only one slice of a freshly made cake.

RICOTTA AND DARK CHOCOLATE ICE CREAM CAKE

The chocolate layers of this dramatic and delectable party piece are a cooked flourless cake. The ice cream is like a very light cheesecake. Although I make this with marmalade, apricot preserves is an excellent alternative.

FOR THE CHOCOLATE LAYERS:
   3 tablespoons water
   5 ounces darkest bitter chocolate, broken into pieces
   4 large eggs
   ¾ cup superfine sugar
   ½ teaspoon salt
   2 tablespoons fine-cut marmalade or apricot preserves
FOR THE ICE CREAM:
   2 egg whites
   1 teaspoon salt
   ¾ cup water
   Scant 1 cup superfine sugar
   ½ cup ricotta cheese
   ½ cup sour cream
   1 square of chocolate, grated

◄ *Ricotta and dark chocolate ice cream cake*

Make the chocolate layers in advance. Line two 8½–9-inch cake pans with a piece of waxed paper. Put the water into a double boiler or a bowl set over a pan of very hot but not boiling water. Add the chocolate. Occasionally stir until the chocolate has melted. Remove the pan from the heat. Now separate the eggs into two large bowls. Add the sugar to the egg yolks and whisk them until pale. Then add the melted chocolate and whisk again until smooth. Add the salt to the egg whites and whisk until they hold soft peaks. Fold the egg whites into the chocolate mixture with a metal spoon and spread the mixture evenly in the cake pans. Cook in the center of a preheated oven, 350°, for about 20 minutes, or until the cakes are firm to touch. Leave to cool in the pans.

When the cakes are cold, loosen the edges of one cake with a knife. Turn it out on to a wide serving plate and remove the paper. Spread the cake thinly with one tablespoon of the marmalade or preserve.

To make the ice cream, put the egg whites into a bowl with the salt and whisk until they hold soft peaks. Put the water and sugar into a saucepan. Stir over a low heat to dissolve the sugar, then bring the mixture to the boil and boil fiercely, without stirring, for three minutes. Then pour the syrup on to the whisked egg whites in a thin stream, whisking all the time. Continue whisking until the mixture is cold and stiff. Lightly whisk together the ricotta and sour cream until smooth and gently fold into the egg white mixture. Spread half the creamy mixture in a thick layer on top of the marmalade-coated chocolate layer.

Loosen the edges of the second cake, turn it out and spread it with the remaining marmalade. Place the cake on top of the layer of ice cream. Spread the remaining ice cream evenly over the top. Finally, sprinkle the grated chocolate on top. Freeze the cake for several hours. An hour before eating, move the cake into the main part of the refrigerator to soften slightly.

UPSIDE-DOWN APPLE TART
WITH ORANGE AND OATMEAL PASTRY

This upside-down tart combines apple with the wonderfully compatible flavors of cardamom, honey and orange, and the oatmeal gives the pastry a nutty crunch. The tart can be made in advance, kept in the cake pan and reheated. I sometimes use a shallow heart-shaped pan which looks especially pretty for a party. If you can find them, quinces make a wonderful substitute for the apples but they will need to be cooked for a little while longer.

1½ cups all-purpose flour
½ cup fine oatmeal
½ cup superfine sugar
¼ teaspoon salt
1 stick butter
Finely grated zest of 1 orange
1–2 tablespoons freshly squeezed
*   orange juice*
1½ pounds apples
4 tablespoons lemon juice
2 tablespoons fine-cut orange
*   marmalade*
2 tablespoons clear honey
Seeds of 4–5 cardamom pods, finely
*   ground*

To make the pastry, put the flour, oatmeal, sugar and salt into a food processor and process just once to mix. Cut the butter into small pieces, add to the flour mixture in the food processor and process again only briefly, just until the mixture resembles rough breadcrumbs. Add the finely grated orange zest and, with the motor running, pour in enough orange juice, processing very briefly, for the dough to begin to stick together. Pat the pastry into a ball, cover it with plastic wrap and leave it in the refrigerator to chill while you prepare the apples.

Smear a little butter over the base and sides of a 7½–8-inch cake pan (don't use a pan with a loose base). Peel the apples, and, using a very sharp knife, cut each apple in half and cut out the cores. Slice the apples thinly in half-moon slices. Put the slices into a bowl and sprinkle them immediately with lemon juice as you cut them to prevent them discoloring.

Put the marmalade and honey into a bowl with the ground cardamom seeds, stir together, and spread the mixture over the bottom of the buttered cake pan. Next, arrange the apple slices neatly overlapping in the pan.

Take the pastry from the refrigerator and, using a well-floured rolling pin, roll it out very lightly on a floured board to the size of the cake pan. Carefully roll back the pastry over the rolling pin and place it on top of the apples in the pan. If the pastry should break at all, don't worry, simply press it together again. Press the overlapping pastry edge down into the sides of the pan and pierce two holes in the top to allow the steam to escape.

Cook the tart in the center of a preheated oven, 400°, for 25 minutes, then turn the oven down to 325° for 30 minutes. Finally, turn off the oven, open the door slightly and leave the tart in the warm oven for a further 10–15 minutes before removing it. *TO SERVE* Slide a knife around the edges of the cake pan and carefully turn the tart out, upside-down, on to a flat serving plate. Serve the tart warm with crème fraîche, cream or plain yogurt, either as a dessert or for a luxurious tea party.
Serves 8

APRICOT, ROSEMARY AND HONEY SOUFFLÉ

Some desserts are truly divine, and this is one of them. It is a very light, chilled soufflé with the wonderful intense flavor of apricots, excitingly enhanced with fresh rosemary. It is marvellously refreshing after a rich meal. You can make it in one large soufflé dish or in six individual ramekins.

12 ounces fresh apricots, finely
*   chopped*
3 tablespoons clear honey
8 tablespoons lemon juice
2 rounded teaspoons finely chopped
*   fresh rosemary*
3 teaspoons powdered gelatin
4 large eggs, separated
Pinch salt
Sprigs whole fresh rosemary, to
*   garnish*

Put the chopped apricots into a saucepan with the honey, lemon juice and chopped rosemary. Bring the mixture up to boiling point, stirring as the honey melts into the apricot mixture, then simmer gently, stirring now and then, for 15–20 minutes or until the apricots have cooked to a soft mush. Remove the pan from the heat and sprinkle the gelatin powder on to the mixture. Stir for a few minutes to allow the powder to dissolve completely into the apricot mixture.

Place the egg yolks in a ceramic bowl set over a pan of barely simmering water. Using a wooden spoon, stir the apricot mixture briskly into the egg yolks. Continue stirring all the time for about five minutes or until the mixture thickens slightly. Then remove the bowl from the heat and set the mixture aside until it has cooled.

When the mixture is cool, place the egg whites into a large bowl, add the salt and whisk until the egg whites hold soft peaks. Using a large metal spoon, fold them gently but thoroughly into the apricot and egg yolk mixture. Pour the mixture into individual dishes or a single serving bowl.

Put a small sprig of rosemary in the center of each individual dish and chill in the refrigerator for at least two hours before serving as an impressive after-dinner dessert.
Serves 6

▶ *Upside-down apple tart with orange and oatmeal pastry; apricot, rosemary and honey soufflé*

RASPBERRY AND ORANGE PARFAIT IN A CHOCOLATE CASE

Years ago, I invented a chocolate case like this for a lemon soufflé. It was such a success that I have done it many times, using different shapes and fillings. This is one of the best. The case is filled with an especially light ice cream. When you can't get raspberries, you can use strawberries instead, and for the best results, use blood orange juice if it's available. Although this recipe uses white chocolate, you can also use dark dessert chocolate. In either case, try to find chocolate with the highest cocoa solid content you can, and no lower than 50%.

FOR THE CHOCOLATE CASE:
> 6 ounces white chocolate
> 1 tablespoon water
> 1 tablespoon sweet butter

FOR THE PARFAIT:
> 1 pound fresh raspberries
> 2 tablespoons clear honey
> Generous ½ cup freshly squeezed
>   orange juice
> Scant 1 cup superfine sugar
> 2 large egg whites
> ¼ teaspoon salt
> 1¼ cups whipping cream
> Mint leaves, to garnish

To make the chocolate case, oil a false-bottom 8-inch deep cake pan. Break up the chocolate and put it with the water into a double saucepan or a bowl set over a pan of hot, but not boiling, water. Stir until the chocolate has melted. Stir in the butter. Spoon the chocolate into the base of the pan and spread it evenly up the sides of the pan, but leaving a very uneven jagged edge. Chill the chocolate case in the refrigerator while you make the parfait.

For the parfait, remove three or four of the best raspberries for the garnish, and keep them in the refrigerator. Press the remaining raspberries through a strainer into a bowl. Stir in the clear honey and leave the purée aside. Strain the orange juice through a strainer into a saucepan and add the sugar. Put the pan over a low heat and stir until the sugar has dissolved; then increase the heat and boil fiercely, without stirring, for three minutes exactly. Meanwhile, put the egg whites into a large bowl with the salt and, using an electric mixer, whisk until they stand in soft peaks. Immediately pour the hot orange syrup on to the whisked egg

whites, whisking all the time. Continue whisking until the mixture is as thick as an uncooked meringue. Lightly stir in the raspberry purée. Whisk the cream until it holds soft peaks, but is not stiff, and fold it into the mixture with a large metal spoon.

Pour the raspberry cream into the chilled chocolate case, piling the mixture up slightly in the center. Freeze the parfait for at least five hours or preferably overnight.

To unmold, rub the sides of the frozen pan with a very hot cloth. Then pass a small spatula down the side of the chocolate and the pan until it has loosened all round. Put the cake pan on a jar and carefully push the sides of the pan down. Separate the chocolate case from the base of the pan with a spatula and carefully move it on to a serving plate. If you are not serving the dessert immediately, re-freeze it until it is needed, although you can keep it in the main part of the refrigerator for about 30 minutes. Just before serving, garnish the parfait with the reserved raspberries and the mint leaves.
Serves 8

BANANA, LEMON AND CARDAMOM ICE CREAM

Ever since I first went to India in 1977, I have been using cardamom for both desserts and ice creams as well as in spiced main dishes. It is truly a wonder spice with amazing versatility, and in desserts it can create a particularly ethereal effect.

> 5 cardamom pods
> 3 large eggs
> ½ teaspoon salt
> 1 cup brown sugar
> 6 tablespoons water
> 4 large ripe bananas, roughly
>   chopped
> Finely grated zest and juice of
>   2 lemons
> 1¼ cups whipping cream

◄ *Raspberry and orange parfait in a
chocolate case*

Remove the seeds from the cardamom pods and grind them finely. Put the eggs, salt and cardamom into the bowl and, using an electric mixer, whisk until frothy. Stir the sugar and water in a saucepan over a low heat until the sugar has dissolved. Then boil fiercely without stirring for three minutes. Pour this bubbling syrup in a thin stream on to the whisked eggs, whisking all the time at high speed. Continue whisking until the mixture thickens. Leave aside to cool.

Put the bananas into a bowl or food processor with the lemon juice and grated lemon zest and mash to a purée. Stir in the cooled egg mixture. Finally, whisk the cream until it is thick but not stiff and fold it into the mixture. Pour the ice cream into a bowl and put it in the freezer for at least three hours.

Move the ice cream to the refrigerator to soften for 30 minutes before serving.
Serves 8

▲ *Banana, lemon and cardamom ice cream*

FRUIT
IN PASSION FRUIT CREAM

This is a lovely mixture using a selection of seasonal berries with contrasting textures and tastes, enveloped in a mixture of crème fraîche, yogurt and ricotta, enhanced by the magic taste of passion fruit.

8 ounces crème fraîche
8 ounces ricotta
3 tablespoons Greek yogurt
½ cup confectioner's sugar
5–6 passion fruit
4 small bananas (optional)
15 ounces seasonal berries, kiwi
    fruit and/or grapes
2 teaspoons clear honey

Put the crème fraîche, ricotta and Greek yogurt into a mixing bowl. Sift in the confectioner's sugar and mix them all together thoroughly.

Cut the passion fruit in half, and scoop out the insides on to the sweetened crème fraîche, ricotta and yogurt mixture. Stir thoroughly to blend in the passion fruit. Peel the bananas, if you are using them, and cut them into small cubes. Immediately stir the banana cubes into the creamy mixture in the bowl.

Prepare the fruit as necessary: choose from raspberries, small strawberries, blueberries, kiwi fruit,

even green or purple grapes; or *fraises des bois* are a really special treat if you can get them. It is good to use fruit with a mildly acidic taste, particularly if you are using banana; it provides a clean, sharp contrast to the luscious sweetness of the banana.

Reserve some of the prettiest fruit for decoration and mix the rest thoroughly into the passion fruit-flavored cream in the bowl.
TO SERVE Spoon the mixture into a pretty glass serving bowl and decorate with the reserved fruit. Drizzle the honey over the top.
Serves 6

CREAMY MARBLED BLACKBERRY
AND YOGURT MOUSSE

This jellied mousse is a delicious combination of puréed and whole fresh blackberries, mingling with a luscious mixture of plain yogurt and whipped heavy cream. The marbled appearance always impresses people. Because the mousse has a beautifully dark, glossy top when it is turned out, be sure to make it in an appropriately-shaped mold. If you like, the mousse can be served with pouring cream.

1½ pounds blackberries
8 tablespoons lemon juice
½ cup superfine sugar
2 tablespoons water
1 tablespoon powdered gelatin
2 large egg whites
½ teaspoon salt
1 cup heavy cream
¾ cup plain yogurt
1 tablespoon confectioner's sugar,
    sifted

Pick out 8 ounces of the best blackberries and put aside. Place the remainder in a pan. Add the lemon juice and superfine sugar, and stir over a gentle heat until the blackberry juices start to run. Then continue to cook

them gently for a few minutes until the blackberries are quite soft. Strain the blackberries into a mixing bowl, pressing the flesh through the strainer with the back of a spoon.

Place the water in a small saucepan over a low heat. Sprinkle the gelatin into the water and stir until it has totally dissolved. Then stir the gelatin mixture thoroughly into the hot blackberry purée. Leave the mixture until it is cold, but only just beginning to set.

Stir the reserved uncooked blackberries into the cold purée. In a separate, clean bowl, whisk the egg whites and salt together until they form soft peaks. Then, using a metal spoon, fold the beaten egg whites gently into the blackberry purée.

In another bowl, whisk the heavy cream until it is thick but has still retained its pouring consistency. Fold the yogurt and confectioner's sugar into the whisked cream. Stir this cream only very roughly into the fruit mixture, leaving large streaks of white.

Lightly oil a 4-cup mold and pour in the unmixed purée and cream into it. Chill the mousse in the refrigerator for at least one hour or until the mousse is well set.

TO SERVE Before serving, turn the mousse out on to a serving plate, giving it a good shake to unmold. If necessary, dip the mold briefly in a sink of hot water to loosen it. Place the mousse back in the refrigerator until you are ready to eat.
Serves 6–8

▲ *Creamy marbled blackberry and yogurt mousse*

◄ *Fruit in passion fruit cream*

131

FROTHY PLUM AND ORANGE CARDAMOM MOUSSE

This mousse makes an interesting change from fresh fruit as a low-fat dessert, and it is prettier too. The mixture separates into a honeycomb mousse with a clear set top. It is best served with cream or yogurt.

1½ pounds red plums, halved and
   pitted
½ cup superfine sugar
1 teaspoon ground cardamom
2 tablespoons plus generous ½ cup
   fresh orange juice
4½ teaspoons powdered gelatin
3 egg whites
½ teaspoon salt
Small fresh mint leaves, to garnish

Place the halved plums into a saucepan with the sugar, cardamom and the two tablespoons of orange juice. Put the pan over a fairly low heat and stir until the sugar dissolves and the plum juices begin to run. Then allow the mixture to bubble gently until the plums are really soft. Remove the pan from the heat. Heat the remaining orange juice in a small saucepan to boiling point, then remove the pan from the heat, and sprinkle in the gelatin. Stir the orange juice until the gelatin has completely dissolved and add it to the plums. Pour the plum mixture into a food processor and process to a fine purée. Turn the mixture into a bowl and leave to cool.

When the plum mixture has cooled, whisk the egg whites with the salt in a clean bowl until they hold soft peaks. Fold the egg whites gently but thoroughly into the cooled plum mixture, using a large metal spoon. Lastly, spoon the mixture into a 4-cup mold. Chill the mold in the refrigerator for several hours until the mousse is set. Before serving, dip the mold briefly in hot water to loosen it and turn out the mousse on to a pretty serving plate.
TO SERVE Decorate the mousse with small mint leaves, or add a small leaf to each individual serving if you prefer.
Serves 8

CHOCOLATE INSPIRATION

I have a real passion for chocolate. In my experience everyone seems to like chocolate desserts so I am always trying to think up new ones. It's important for this one that the chocolate should be as dark and bitter as possible.

6 ounces dark dessert chocolate
6 tablespoons water
8 ounces slightly stale unsliced
   white bread
Juice of 5 lemons
1 cup brown sugar
1 rounded tablespoon honey
3 tablespoons brandy

Line an 8-inch cake pan with waxed paper, generously overlapping the edge. Break up half the chocolate into the top of a double boiler or a bowl set over a pan of hot but not boiling water – the bowl should not touch the water. Add three tablespoons of the water and stir occasionally until the chocolate is melted and smooth. Allow it to cool slightly, then pour into the lined pan. Using a spatula, spread the chocolate evenly, being sure not to leave any gaps, up the sides to the edge of the pan and over the bottom. Put the cake

◀ *Frothy plum and orange cardamom mousse*

pan into the refrigerator for 30 minutes to allow the chocolate case to harden.

Meanwhile, slice the bread into thick slices and cut off the crusts. Lay the bread slices, touching each other closely, in one layer in a shallow dish. Put the lemon juice into a measuring container and, if necessary, bring up the quantity of liquid to 2 cups with water. Pour the liquid into a saucepan and add the brown sugar and the honey. Put the saucepan over a medium heat and stir until the sugar and honey have dissolved, then boil the liquid fiercely, without stirring, for two minutes. Remove the pan from the heat and stir in the brandy to taste.

Gradually spoon half the syrup evenly over the slices of bread, allowing it to absorb thoroughly. Turn the soaked slices of bread over and spoon on the remaining syrup. Leave the soaked bread on one side until it has cooled completely and absorbed all the syrup.

When the chocolate has been in the refrigerator for at least 30 minutes and the bread has absorbed the syrup and is quite cold, lay the bread in the chocolate case. Then break up the remaining half of the chocolate and put it into the bowl previously used with the remaining water. Set the bowl over

a pan of hot water. Stir the chocolate until it is melted and smooth; then spoon it on top of the soaked bread and spread it all over evenly and up the sides of the chocolate case to enclose the bread. Put the pan in the freezer for about one hour; then turn the cake upside down on to a serving plate and peel off the paper.
TO SERVE Leave the cake at room temperature for one hour before serving.
Serves 6

▲ *Chocolate inspiration*

HONEY-GLAZED FRESH APRICOT TART

Fresh apricots bought in the stores have often been picked before they are ripe, and their flavor is nearly always improved by cooking. This honeyed upside-down cake (which I also make with apples) is particularly successful. The pastry is easy and does not even need rolling, as you lay thin pieces over the fruit like a patchwork and it cooks into the most delicious, buttery pastry base when the tart is turned out.

2½ pounds fresh firm apricots
½ cup brown sugar
1½ cups all-purpose flour
1 cup confectioner's sugar
½ teaspoon salt
1 stick butter
Finely grated zest and juice of
    1 lemon
1 tablespoon clear honey
    (approximately), warmed

Cut the apricots in half and remove the pits. Spoon the brown sugar into a well-buttered 12-inch earthenware pie plate and shake to an even layer on the base. Arrange a layer of apricots neatly in circles, skin side down, over the sugar in the dish. Cut any remaining apricots into smaller pieces and arrange them on top of the first layer, filling in any holes with the smallest pieces.

Sift the flour, confectioner's sugar and salt into a bowl. Melt the butter in a saucepan with the lemon zest and juice, and then pour the juices gradually into the flour mixture, mixing as you pour, until you have a soft dough. Take pieces of the dough, press them out between the palms of your hands into fairly thin pieces and lay them on top of the apricots until the whole tart is covered. Patch any holes with little bits of pastry and press the

pastry down into the dish at the edges. Then put the tart in the refrigerator for at least 30 minutes.

Using a skewer, pierce four holes in the pastry to allow the steam to escape. Cook the tart in the center of a preheated oven, 425°, for 25 minutes or until the pastry has browned. Turn down the heat to 300° and continue cooking for another 30 minutes. Turn off the heat but leave the tart in the oven for about 15 minutes.

While still warm, loosen the edges of the tart with a knife, put a large serving plate on top of the pie plate and turn the tart upside down to unmold, revealing the apricots. Brush the warmed honey all over the apricots.
TO SERVE Serve the tart warm, if possible, and on its own or with fresh cream or Greek yogurt.
Serves 8–10

CLEAR RHUBARB AND RED WINE MOLD FLAVORED WITH GINGER

Even people who say they don't like rhubarb welcome this refreshing dessert with enthusiasm after a large meal. When they are in season, flavoring the dessert with a few heads of fresh elder-flower adds a wonderfully scented flavor and you can also use them to decorate it, if you like.

½ pound rhubarb
1-inch piece fresh root ginger
2–3 elderflower heads (optional)
¼ cup granulated sugar
4 tablespoons lemon juice
Juice of 2 oranges
1¼ cups red wine
2 tablespoons water
4 teaspoons powdered gelatin

Cut the rhubarb and ginger into rough pieces. Put both these ingredients into a large saucepan. Wash the elderflower heads, if using, before pulling off the flowers and adding them to the saucepan together with the sugar. Using a fine strainer, strain the lemon

and orange juice into the mixture, followed by the red wine. Put the pan over the heat, bring the mixture to the boil and then allow it to simmer gently for about 15 minutes or until the rhubarb is completely mushy. Remove the pan from the heat and strain the liquid into a mixing bowl. Then strain the liquid back through the finest strainer into another bowl or clean saucepan.

Put the water into a separate saucepan, bring it up to boiling and then remove the pan from the heat. Then sprinkle in the gelatin and stir until the powder is completely dissolved. Stir the gelatin mixture into the strained rhubarb and wine liquid. Pour the mixture into a 4½-cup metal gelatin dessert mold or into individual molds and leave until cold. Then put it in the refrigerator to set.

Before serving, dip the mold briefly in hot water and turn the dessert out on to a serving plate, giving it a shake against the plate to release it.
TO SERVE Decorate the dessert around the edge with sprigs of

elderflower or rose petals, or whatever edible flowers are available.
Serves 4

▲ *Clear rhubarb and red wine mold flavored with ginger*

◀ *Honey-glazed fresh apricot tart*

VANISHING SOUFFLÉ
WITH CHOCOLATE BRANDY CUSTARD

This is a steamed, sweetened egg white soufflé which literally does vanish in your mouth. Pure white, it is served with a chocolate brandy custard.

> *4 large eggs, separated*
> *⅓ cup plus 1 tablespoon superfine sugar*
> *1 tablespoon brandy*
> *Generous ½ cup heavy cream*
> *2 squares dark dessert chocolate, grated*

In a clean bowl, whisk the egg whites until thick, then whisk in ⅓ cup of the sugar. Continue whisking until the mixture stands in stiff peaks. Spoon the egg white into a soufflé dish; then put the dish into a large, deep saucepan filled with hot water (the soufflé will rise spectacularly) so that the hot water comes three-quarters of the way up the sides of the dish. Cover the saucepan and cook over the lowest possible heat (do not even allow the water to simmer) for 1½ hours.

Meanwhile make the sauce. Whisk the egg yolks in a bowl with the remaining 1 tablespoon of sugar and the brandy. Place the cream in a pouring saucepan and bring it to a rolling boil, then pour it immediately on to the egg yolks, whisking swiftly all the time. Whisk in the grated chocolate thoroughly, then leave the custard to cool. Once it has cooled down, chill the brandy custard in the refrigerator.

When the soufflé is ready, remove the soufflé dish from the pan, allow it to cool and then chill the soufflé in the refrigerator. During chilling, it may shrink quite a lot.

TO SERVE On individual plates, pour a pool of custard. Using a large serving spoon, take up a heaped spoonful of the soufflé and place on the pool of custard.
Serves 5–6

SHARP LEMON SOUFFLÉ
ON A CHOCOLATE SHORTBREAD BASE

This is a wonderfully light and frothy hot soufflé. People often think it is impractical to make a soufflé for the end of the meal but as this is made in stages, almost all of it can be done well in advance. All you have left to do at the end is fold in the egg whites just before cooking. Since the actual cooking takes approximately one hour, this means that the soufflé will be ready just about the time you finish the first part of the meal. During the summer season, a bowl full of fresh ripe raspberries is a perfect accompaniment.

FOR THE CHOCOLATE SHORTBREAD:
> *1¼ cups all-purpose flour*
> *¼ cup cocoa powder*
> *½ teaspoon salt*
> *3 rounded tablespoons superfine sugar*
> *1¼ sticks soft butter*

FOR THE SOUFFLÉ:
> *4 large eggs*
> *Scant ½ cup superfine sugar*
> *Generous ½ cup freshly squeezed lemon juice (3–4 lemons)*
> *Finely grated zest of 2 lemons*
> *Salt*

To make the chocolate shortbread, butter a 9-inch china pie plate. Sift the flour, cocoa, salt and sugar together into a bowl. Work the butter into the flour mixture with your fingertips. Then, using floured hands, gather the dough together and press it lightly but evenly over the bottom of the pie plate. Prick the base of the shortbread all over with a fork and put it in the refrigerator for at least 20 minutes. Cook the chocolate shortbread in the center of a preheated oven, 400°, for 15–20 minutes. Remove from the oven and leave it to cool.

While the shortbread is cooking, begin to make the soufflé. Separate the eggs. Put the egg yolks into the top of a double saucepan or a bowl set over a pan of hot water. Put the whites into a large whisking bowl. Stir the sugar into the egg yolks and then, a little at a time, add the lemon juice. Put the saucepan over a medium heat and stir all the time until it has thickened to make a lemon custard which coats the back of the spoon. Stir in the grated lemon zest and leave the custard to cool.

Add a pinch of salt to the egg whites and whisk the whites until they hold soft peaks. Then, using a metal spoon, lightly fold the cooled lemon custard into the egg whites. Pile the mixture on top of the shortbread base. Cook the soufflé towards the top of a preheated oven, 300°, for 50 minutes to 1 hour until browned.

TO SERVE Serve the soufflé with berries and/or cream, crème fraîche or yogurt.
Serves 6

◄ *Vanishing soufflé with chocolate brandy custard*

▲ *Sharp lemon soufflé on a chocolate shortbread base*

CARROT TART WITH CANDIED CARROT TOPPING

This foolproof recipe is based on the description of a tart I once read in a Victorian book. The glossy orange top gives it a most striking appearance.

FOR THE PASTRY:
  1¼ cups all-purpose flour
  ½ teaspoon salt
  ½ cup confectioner's sugar
  1 egg
  ¾ stick soft butter
FOR THE FILLING:
  ½ stick butter
  2 eggs
  2 egg yolks
  1 cup light cream or milk
  Generous ½ cup superfine sugar
  1 cup fresh white breadcrumbs
  Finely grated zest of 1 lemon
  1 cup grated carrot
  ½ whole nutmeg, grated
FOR THE TOPPING:
  8 ounces carrots
  Scant 1 cup white granulated sugar
  4 tablespoons lemon juice
  4 tablespoons water

Make the pastry in advance. Sift the flour, salt and confectioner's sugar into a mixing bowl. Make a well in the center. Whisk the egg lightly with a fork and drop it in. Then add the butter and work the mixture together with your hands until it is well blended, about 1–2 minutes. Dust your hands with flour and knead the dough lightly with the palms of your hands until you have a smooth ball of dough. Wrap the dough in plastic wrap and chill for at least one hour.

To make the filling, melt the butter and leave it to cool slightly. In a mixing bowl, whisk together the eggs, egg yolks, melted butter, cream and the sugar. Stir in the breadcrumbs, lemon zest, grated carrot and nutmeg.

Butter a 10–10½-inch false-bottomed fluted tart pan. Roll out the chilled pastry on a well-floured surface into a circle a little bigger than the pan. Line the pan with the pastry, turning the slightly overlapping edges in again to make a neat thick edge. Prick the base of the pastry case all over with a fork. Pour the prepared filling into the pastry case. Bake the tart in the center of a preheated oven, 350°, for 45–50 minutes or until the filling is golden and has risen slightly.

Finally, to make the topping, peel the carrots and slice them into roughly 2-inch long julienne strips (use the special blade of the food processor for this if you have one). Put the strips into a saucepan with the sugar, lemon juice and water over a medium heat. Stir to dissolve the sugar, then increase the heat and boil briskly for about five minutes or until a blob of syrup sets on a cold saucer. Remove the pan from the heat and allow the topping to cool slightly before spreading it all over the top of the tart. Serve the tart either warm or at room temperature. Before serving, put the pan on a jar and carefully push the sides down. Using a wide spatula, carefully ease the tart off the base on to a large flat serving plate.
Serves 8

WHITE PEAR CAKE

This white-crumbed cake is topped with pear slices spiced with cinnamon. It can be served warm with cream or yogurt as a dessert, or eaten cold for a delicious snack. It can also be made with apples.

  ½ stick soft butter
  3 tablespoons soft light brown sugar
  Finely grated zest of 2 lemons
  2 teaspoons ground cinnamon
  1 pound firm pears
  1½ cups all-purpose flour
  2 teaspoons baking powder
  ½ teaspoon salt
  6 tablespoons sunflower oil
  8 tablespoons lemon juice
  6 tablespoons milk
  2 large egg whites
  Pinch cream of tartar
  Scant 1 cup superfine sugar

Spread the butter thickly over the bottom and rather more thinly up the sides of a 9-inch cake pan. Mix the light brown sugar together with the lemon zest and cinnamon. Spread two-thirds of this sugar mixture over the butter on the bottom of the pan. Peel the pears, cut them into thin slices and overlap them on top of the sugar in the pan, using them all up. Sprinkle the remaining cinnamon sugar on top.

Sift the flour, baking powder and salt into a bowl. Pour in the oil. Strain in the lemon juice and add the milk. Beat this mixture together until you have a rather thick, smooth batter. In a separate bowl, whisk the egg whites until foamy. Add the cream of tartar and whisk again until the mixture is stiff but not breaking up. Gradually whisk in the sugar. Using a metal spoon, fold the mixture into the batter and then pour it on top of the pears. Cook the cake in the center of a preheated oven, 350°, for 50 minutes to 1 hour. Leave the cake in the pan for about 10 minutes; then turn it out, upside-down, on to a serving plate.

◀ *Carrot tart with candied carrot topping*

▲ *White pear cake*

ROSE PETAL SHERBET WITH CRYSTALIZED PETALS

The petals of heavily scented roses have a unique flavor for which I developed a passion during my childhood in the Middle East. Later on I was reacquainted with it in the delectable rose petal preserves of Turkey, and in many Indian candies. After a large meal, this romantic sherbet is the perfect light and reviving finale.

FOR THE SHERBET:
   Petals of 4 heavily scented red roses
   2 cups water
   3½ cups superfine sugar
   4 tablespoons lemon juice
   ½–1 tablespoon rose water
      (available in Middle Eastern or
      gourmet food stores)
   2 large egg whites
   ¼ teaspoon salt
FOR THE CRYSTALIZED PETALS:
   1 large egg white
   Petals of 1 large heavily scented red
      rose
   Superfine sugar

To make the sherbet, wash the rose petals and put them in a saucepan with the water. Bring the water to the boil, cover the pan and simmer the petals gently for 10 minutes. Remove the pan from the heat and strain the water into another saucepan, reserving the petals. Add the sugar to the strained water and put the pan over a low heat, stirring until the sugar has completely dissolved. Then bring to the boil and boil fiercely, without stirring, for three minutes. Remove from the heat and stir in the lemon juice, and the extra rose water to taste. Then stir in the reserved rose petals and leave until cold.

When the mixture is cold, pour it into a mixing bowl and put it in the freezer. When the sherbet is half-frozen, take it out and break it up to a mush with a fork. In a bowl, whisk the egg whites with the salt until they stand in soft peaks and fold them gently but thoroughly into the rose petal sherbet with a metal spoon. Transfer the

sherbet to a pretty serving bowl – glass looks best – and put it back in the freezer.

Now make the crystalized rose petals. Put a piece of waxed paper on a large baking tray. Whisk the egg white until stiff but not breaking up. Paint each rose petal lightly with egg white, then dip it in the bowl of sugar, shaking off the excess. Lay the coated petals on the waxed paper. Put them in a warm dry place for 1–1½ hours or until the petals are quite dry and crisp. Then carefully peel the petals off the paper. If you are not going to eat the sherbet for several hours, or until the next day, keep the petals in an air-tight container – they must be kept absolutely dry.

Shortly before serving, scatter a few crystalized petals on the sherbet. Put the remaining crystalized petals into a pretty bowl on the table for your guests to scatter on to their individual serving.
Serves 6

GODDESS OF PUDDINGS

Along with bread and butter pudding, "queen of puddings" is a justly famous old-fashioned English classic dessert, and one which I love. This variation, which I make with citrus zest and orange marmalade instead of the red preserves used in "queen of puddings", is to me even better. It can be served with cream, and either hot or cold.

   1½ cups fresh white breadcrumbs
   2 cups milk
   Finely grated zest of 2 medium-sized
      oranges
   Juice and finely grated zest of
      1 lemon
   ½ stick butter
   3 large eggs, separated
   Generous ½ cup light brown sugar
   4 rounded tablespoons orange
      marmalade
   ¼ teaspoon salt

Butter an oval or rectangular ovenproof dish. Spread the breadcrumbs over the bottom of the dish. Put the milk into a saucepan and add the finely grated zest of one orange and the lemon. Add the butter and stir over a low heat until the butter has melted and the mixture is just warm. Put the egg yolks into a mixing bowl. Add a scant ½ cup sugar and whisk together lightly. Then gradually stir in the heated milk and butter. Pour this mixture over the breadcrumbs in the dish. Bake the custard in the center of a preheated oven, 350°, for about 25 minutes or until the custard has set to a light touch in the center. Then remove the custard from the oven. Mix the lemon juice into the marmalade and spread the mixture over the top. In a clean bowl, whisk the egg whites with the salt until they stand in soft peaks. Using a metal spoon, fold the remaining sugar and the finely grated zest of the remaining orange into the egg whites. Pile this

meringue over the marmalade and sprinkle a very little extra sugar over the top. Return the pudding to the oven for 10–15 minutes or until golden.
Serves 6

▲ *Goddess of puddings*

◄ *Rose petal sherbet with crystalized petals*

CHOCOLATE CAKE WITH VANILLA AND CINNAMON

A very chocolaty cake with a delicate crumb, this is equally good as a dessert with soft berries or cream.

6 squares dark dessert chocolate
1 stick soft butter
¾ cup superfine sugar
3 teaspoons vanilla
2 teaspoons ground cinnamon
4 large eggs, separated
2 tablespoons self-raising flour
1 tablespoon cocoa powder
Pinch salt
Confectioner's sugar, to decorate

Butter a deep 6½–7-inch cake pan. Line the bottom with buttered waxed paper. Dust the pan with flour. Melt the chocolate in a bowl set over a pan of very hot but not boiling water, stirring until the chocolate has melted. Whisk together the butter and sugar until soft and fluffy. Then whisk in the melted chocolate, the vanilla, the cinnamon and the egg yolks. Sift the flour and cocoa powder on to the mixture and lightly whisk in.

Whisk the egg whites with the salt until they hold soft peaks. Fold them into the chocolate mixture. Turn the mixture into the cake pan and cook in the center of a preheated oven, 350°, for about 40 minutes, or until the cake has risen and a crust has formed on top. Don't pierce to test it.

Leave the cake in the pan for 10 minutes, then turn it out upside down on to a cake rack and remove the waxed paper. Finally, turn the cake right side up (it may sink a little) and sift or sprinkle confectioner's sugar over the top. Transfer the cake on to a serving plate.

SQUIDGY PRUNE, PECAN, CITRUS AND HONEY CAKE

This uses the old-fashioned method of boiling the ingredients before baking.

1½ sticks butter
1¼ cups soft brown sugar
1¼ cups water
8 ounces pitted prunes, chopped
2 ounces stem ginger, chopped
Coarsely grated zest and juice of
* 1 orange and 1 lemon*
Generous 1 cup pecan pieces
2 cups all-purpose flour
1 teaspoon baking soda
1 teaspoon ground cinnamon
2 large eggs
1 tablespoon honey
Half pecans, to decorate

Grease a deep 6–7-inch cake pan and line the bottom with waxed paper. In a saucepan, dissolve the butter and sugar in the water. Place the prunes, ginger, orange and lemon zest and nuts into the saucepan. Bring to the boil, cover, and simmer gently for 10–15 minutes. Leave to cool. Sift the flour and baking soda into a mixing bowl and add the cinnamon; then stir in the cool fruit mixture with a wooden spoon. In a separate bowl, whisk the eggs until frothy and mix them thoroughly into the fruit mixture.

Pour the cake mixture into the prepared pan, and place half pecans all over the top. Bake in the center of a preheated oven, 350°, for about 1 1/4 hours, or until a knife inserted in the center of the cake comes out clean.

Using a fine skewer, pierce the warm cake all over through to the bottom. Put the honey into a small saucepan and strain in the orange and lemon juice. Stir to dissolve the honey over a medium heat, then allow the mixture to bubble fiercely for two minutes. Spoon this syrup slowly over the cake, allowing it to absorb into the skewer holes.

Leave the cake to cool in the pan, then loosen the sides of the cake with a knife and turn it out. Wrap in plastic wrap until ready to eat.

CITRUS-DRENCHED CAKE

2 sticks butter
Generous 1 cup soft light brown
* sugar*
4 large eggs
Zest and juice of 2–3 lemons
½ cup ground almonds
1½ cups self-raising flour
2 teaspoons baking powder
½ teaspoon salt
3 tablespoons fresh orange juice
⅓ cup superfine caster sugar

◄ *Chocolate cake with vanilla and cinnamon; squidgy prune, pecan, citrus and honey cake; citrus-drenched cake*

Butter a 7½-inch cake pan and line it with a piece of buttered waxed paper. Dust the pan with flour. In a large bowl, whisk the butter until soft and then whisk in the brown sugar until fluffy. Thoroughly whisk in one egg at a time. Finely grate the lemon zest and add to the mixture together with the almonds. In a separate bowl, sift together the flour, baking powder and salt and stir this into the egg mixture. Spoon this mixture into the pan and level the top. Cook in the center of a preheated oven, 350°, for 1¼–1½ hours or until the cake is springy to touch, and a knife inserted in the middle comes out clean. If it browns too much, cover the top loosely with foil.

Strain the lemon juice into a saucepan. Add the orange juice and the superfine sugar and stir over a low heat to dissolve the sugar. Then boil fiercely without stirring for two minutes. Pierce the cake, still in its pan, right through all over with a skewer. Spoon the citrus syrup on to it very gradually, allowing the juices to seep into the holes. Leave the cake in the pan until almost cold, then loosen the sides with a knife and turn the cake out.

BREADS, COOKIES & PRESERVES

When putting together a cookbook, there are always odds and ends which don't fit into any of the chapter categories. But to me, they are often things which are so delicious or full of good memories that I just have to put them in somewhere; this is certainly true of my ambrosial apricot preserves flavored with elderflowers. And there is still something particularly special about bread-making. Now that we have easy-blend yeast, which makes bread-making so much less laborious than it used to be, it is tempting to try out all sorts of different breads with added ingredients; they can really be the making of a light lunch or picnic. Basic bread recipes can be adapted in many different ways. Perhaps the breads I have produced will inspire you to try out variations of your own. It is, I find, almost impossible to make the same bread twice. So many exciting and delicious possibilities are offered by the huge range of herbs and spices available nowadays, not to mention cheeses and olives and all the other things you can find on modern delicatessen counters. Children seem to love making bread, cookies and snacks. So I hope that this final little medley will have something to attract cooks of all ages.

KEN BUGGY'S IRISH SODA BREAD

Ken Buggy makes everyone welcome at his charming B & B in Kinsale, Co. Cork, Ireland. Every morning at breakfast his warm, freshly baked soda bread is on the table. This is his own recipe which I have used ever since I spent a happy few days there. In Ireland you can get coarser ground whole wheat flour than elsewhere, which is why in this recipe I grind some wheat grains to achieve the true Irish effect. Soda bread must be eaten very fresh, preferably warm, but since it takes only five minutes to make and 30 minutes to cook, this is easily possible. Ken Buggy stresses that not only should this dough not be kneaded but it should be handled as lightly and briefly as possible when you are gathering it up into a rather rough-looking round loaf.

◀ *Ken Buggy's Irish soda bread*

1 cup whole wheat grains
1 cup stoneground whole wheat
   flour
3 cups strong white flour
2–3 teaspoons crushed sea salt
2 tablespoons bran
1 rounded teaspoon baking soda
1½–2 cups buttermilk

Put the whole wheat grains into an electric coffee grinder and process just until coarsely ground and still bitty. Put these grains into a large mixing bowl and add the stoneground whole wheat flour, the strong white flour, the sea salt, the bran and the baking soda. Using a wooden spoon, mix all these dry ingredients together well.

Then, still using the wooden spoon, gradually and lightly stir in the buttermilk until you have a soft dough which just about sticks together enough to leave the side of the mixing bowl as you stir. Handling the dough very lightly, quickly gather the dough up to form a rough, round ball. Do not knead it at all.

Thoroughly flour a baking tray. Put the ball of dough on to the baking tray and, using a large sharp knife, cut a deep cross almost, but not completely, through the dough.

Place the soda bread on a shelf just above the center of a preheated oven, 450°, and bake it for about 30 minutes: when the bread is ready, it should sound hollow when you tap the underside. Then turn the bread upside down and put it back in the oven for a further 2–3 minutes just to firm up the crust on the base of the loaf. Eat the soda bread while it is still warm, if possible, or at least while it is still very freshly baked.

GREEK SALAD BREAD

A big chunk of this bread, served while it is still warm (or reheated) with a green salad, is a meal in itself. I sometimes include walnut halves in the bread dough, too.

9 tablespoons olive oil
3 medium onions, finely chopped
6 cups strong plain white flour
2 rounded teaspoons crushed sea
*   salt*
3 rounded teaspoons dried oregano
2 teaspoons whole coriander seeds
1 rounded teaspoon green
*   peppercorns*
5 ounces feta cheese, roughly cubed
4 tomatoes, chopped
2 ounces pitted black olives, halved
2 packets easy-blend yeast

Put three tablespoons of the olive oil in a large skillet over a medium high heat. Fry the chopped onion until soft and well browned, stirring often. Then turn the onion into a bowl to cool slightly.

Put the white flour into a large bowl and stir in the sea salt, oregano, coriander seeds and peppercorns. Add the feta cheese, tomatoes, olives and all but a small spoonful of the onion to the mixture. Put the remaining oil into a measuring jug and bring up the liquid to 1½ cups with warm water. Stir the liquid gradually into the bread mixture. Mix in the yeast. Then, using floured hands, gather up the dough and form it into two equal balls. Generously oil two 7–8-inch cake pans. Place one ball of dough in each pan and cut a deep

cross in each. Sprinkle the dough with the reserved onions. Put the pans inside a large plastic garbage bag, puffing the bag up and turning it under the pans to trap the air. Leave the dough at room temperature for about two hours until it is well risen.

Bake the loaves, side by side if possible, in the center of a preheated oven, 450°, for 20 minutes. Then turn down the heat to 400° and cook the loaves for another 20 minutes, or until the bread sounds hollow when tapped. Turn the loaves out on to a rack to cool slightly and eat warm. This bread does not need to be buttered unless you prefer it. If you are taking it on a picnic, wrap it in plenty of newspaper to keep it warm.

ANGLO-SYRIAN BREAD

As a child in Damascus, I remember the flat, unleavened bread being the best I have ever tasted. However, in a conventional loaf, I can incorporate many of the exotic, spicy ingredients and combinations which I started to love in those early Middle Eastern days. This loaf, full of nuts, seeds and spices, is a wonderful accompaniment to a salad lunch. Easy-blend dried yeast makes breadmaking simple enough even for the inexperienced breadmaker. Shelled pistachios are an excellent alternative to the walnuts.

1 large onion, chopped
2 ounces pine nuts
4 cups strong white flour
1 tablespoon crushed sea salt
2 teaspoons cumin seeds
2 teaspoons coriander seeds,
*   roughly crushed*
½ cup sesame seeds
¾ cup walnut pieces, roughly ground
Generous handful mint leaves,
*   roughly chopped*
4 tablespoons extra virgin olive oil
1 packet easy-blend yeast
1 cup water

◂ *Greek salad bread*

Smear a 10 x 2-inch circular earthenware dish or cake pan with olive oil. Put the chopped onion into a dry skillet over a high heat and stir just to darken the pieces of onion. Then add all but one tablespoon of the pine nuts. Toss for a minute just until the pine nuts are browned and remove the pan from the heat. Put the flour and sea salt into a mixing bowl and stir together. Then stir in the cumin and coriander seeds, all but two teaspoons of the sesame seeds, the walnut pieces and the fried onion and pine nuts. Stir the chopped mint into the mixture.

Stir in the olive oil, mix in the yeast and then gradually add the water, just until the mixture sticks together. Then gather up and knead the dough lightly on a floured surface for about five minutes.

Put the dough into the oiled dish or pan. Cut a deep star in the top and scatter with the reserved unbrowned pine nuts and sesame seeds. Cover the dish or pan with a large plastic bag tucked in under the dish, trapping plenty of air and ballooning up above the dough. Leave the dish at room temperature for about two hours or until the dough has doubled in size.

Remove the plastic and place the loaf in the center of a preheated oven, 450°, for 20 minutes; then turn down the heat to 400° and leave the bread to bake for a further 20 minutes. Turn the loaf out of the dish or pan and leave it to cool on a rack.

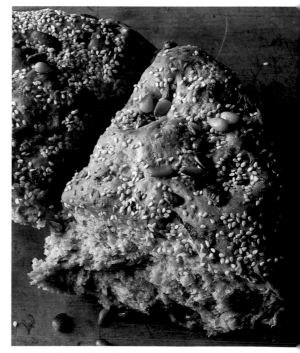

▴ *Anglo-Syrian bread*

ANCHOVY, GARLIC AND PARSLEY STICKS

If you keep ready-made puff pastry in your freezer, and cans of anchovies in the pantry, you can make these appetizing little sticks anytime. They are ideal with drinks before a meal.

2 ounce can anchovies
1 large garlic clove
Generous handful parsley, trimmed
8 ounces puff pastry
1 egg yolk, to glaze
Black pepper
Grated Parmesan cheese, to
    sprinkle

Empty the anchovies, together with their oil, into the bowl of a food processor. Add the garlic and parsley and plenty of black pepper and process as finely as possible.

Divide the pastry in half. Roll out both halves on a flat surface into two rectangles not more than ⅛-inch thick. Spread the anchovy mixture evenly over one rectangle, and then place the other rectangle on top and press down lightly all over.

Using a sharp knife, cut the pastry into sticks about 2 x ¾-inch long.

Grease a large baking tray and arrange the sticks on it. Brush the sticks with the egg yolk to glaze and sprinkle lightly with the Parmesan cheese.

Place the sticks on a shelf just above the center of a preheated oven, 400°, and bake for about 10–15 minutes until the sticks have puffed up and are golden brown.
TO SERVE If possible, serve the sticks warm – you can either keep them warm in a low oven or simply re-heat them when you are ready.
Makes about 24 sticks

ORANGE AND ROSEMARY FINGER COOKIES

This is the most convenient way of being able to produce home-made freshly baked cookies, which always seem like a real treat. You make up the dough, form it into a long roll and keep it in the freezer so that every time you want some cookies, you simply slice as many as you need off the roll and put them straight into the oven on a baking tray. They cook in 10 minutes and keep really well in an airtight container.

1 x 3-inch sprig fresh rosemary
1 stick butter
1 cup superfine sugar
1 large egg
Finely grated zest of 1 large orange
2 cups all-purpose flour
2 teaspoons baking powder
½ teaspoon salt

Pull the rosemary spikes off their stem and chop them as finely as possible. Whisk the butter and sugar together until they have turned a pale, light color. Beat the egg lightly with a fork and whisk it into the butter and sugar thoroughly, a little at a time.

Then stir in the chopped rosemary and grated orange zest. Sift the flour with the baking powder and salt into a bowl. Stir the flour into the butter mixture. Flour your hands and shape the dough into a long, rather flat roll. If you find the dough is too soft to shape easily, refrigerate it briefly until it becomes firmer. Wrap the roll up in plastic wrap and lay it on a flat surface in the freezer.

Whenever you want the cookies, have a large ungreased baking tray

ready. Take the frozen roll of dough from the freezer, and using a sharp knife, slice off the cookies as thinly as you can.

Place the cookies on the baking tray a little apart, as they expand during cooking. Place the baking tray in the center of a preheated oven, 375°, and bake the cookies for 7–9 minutes until they are a pale golden color.

Immediately, while they are still hot, ease the cookies off the tray with a palette knife and put them on a rack to cool. If you want curved cookies, drape them over a rolling pin or any other cylindrical object and leave to cool.
TO SERVE These light and buttery cookies are perfect for parties or with ice cream or fruity desserts.
Makes about 50 cookies

HIGHLAND OATCAKES

I first tasted these lovely oatcakes in the Outer Hebrides off the northwest coast of Scotland. We had them every day, either simply spread with butter or with locally made honey. They are perfect with cheese.

1 cup oatmeal
½ teaspoon salt
Generous pinch baking soda
4 tablespoons water
1 tablespoon butter

Mix together the oatmeal, salt and baking soda in a bowl. Bring the water to the boil in a small saucepan. Add the butter and stir until it has melted. Pour the liquid into the middle of the oat mixture and stir thoroughly until you have a fairly moist dough.

Sprinkle a baking tray thinly with oatmeal. Form the dough into a ball and put it into the center of the baking tray. Using the palm of your hands, press the dough out into a rough 8-inch

circle. Press along the edge to neaten it slightly. Using a sharp knife, score across the circle each way until you have eight triangular-shaped slices. Cook them in the center of a preheated oven, 375°, for 20–25 minutes. Leave on a rack to cool.
Makes 8 cakes

▶ Anchovy, garlic and parsley sticks; orange and rosemary finger cookies; Highland oatcakes

148

TOMATO, HERB, PARMESAN AND GARLIC BREAD WITH OLIVE OIL

I have made many versions of this Italian-style bread, but this one, without olives, has been the most popular of all. Served warm, it makes a light lunch with cheese and salad.

3 cups strong or unbleached all-purpose flour
2 tablespoons crushed sea salt
3 ounces Parmesan cheese
2 large sprigs fresh rosemary
10–12 basil leaves
12–15 sage leaves
10–12 sun-dried tomatoes, thinly sliced
2 large garlic cloves, finely chopped
5 tablespoons extra virgin olive oil
1 packet easy-blend yeast
Water

Oil a large pizza pan or baking tray. Put the flour into a large bowl and stir in all but two teaspoons of the sea salt. Pare off a little Parmesan with a potato peeler for decoration, and grate the remainder. Chop one sprig of rosemary. Thinly slice the basil and all but two of the sage leaves. Add the grated Parmesan, chopped rosemary, sliced basil and sage, sliced sun-dried tomatoes and garlic to the flour. Stir with a wooden spoon, then stir in three tablespoons of the oil. Mix in the yeast, then add enough water to form a slightly sticky, soft dough. Knead on a very lightly floured surface for about five minutes until smooth and elastic.

Form the dough into a ball, then press it out with your hand into a very rough circle about ½–¾-inch thick and 10 inches in diameter. Transfer the dough to the oiled pan and, using a wooden salad fork, prick the surface deeply all over.

Put the pan inside a large plastic bag and fold the bag in under the pan, trapping plenty of air so that it is puffed up well above the bread. Leave at room temperature for about two hours until the dough has doubled in thickness.

Remove the bag and trickle the remaining oil over the bread, spreading it lightly with your fingers and letting it sit in any dips. Sprinkle on the reserved Parmesan, sage, sea salt and whole rosemary. Bake in the center of a preheated oven, 425°, for about 20 minutes or until dark golden brown.

AROMATIC VEGETABLE TURNOVERS WITH YOGURT PASTRY

These are especially good for picnics. The pastry is light and crispy and the turnovers can be eaten cold (but not chilled), although they are nicest warm. Use red onions if available.

FOR THE FILLING:
1 tablespoon butter
2 tablespoons olive oil
8 ounces onions, finely chopped
1 garlic clove, finely chopped
6 ounces potatoes, cut in small cubes
2 teaspoons ground coriander
1 teaspoon ground cumin
1 cup frozen small peas
Handful fresh mint leaves, finely chopped
Salt and black pepper
FOR THE PASTRY:
1 stick butter
1 tablespoon olive oil
1 small egg
½ cup plain yogurt
2½ cups all-purpose flour
¼ teaspoon baking soda
1 teaspoon salt
1 egg yolk

◄ *Tomato, herb, Parmesan and garlic bread with olive oil*

Make the filling first. Melt the butter and olive oil in a large skillet over a medium heat. Add the onions and garlic, and cook for a few minutes, stirring occasionally until the onions begin to soften. Add the cubed potatoes and cook for 5–7 minutes, stirring occasionally, until they too are just soft. Stir in the spices and cook for one minute; then remove the skillet from the heat. Add the peas.

Turn the mixture into a mixing bowl and season it well with salt and pepper. Stir the mint into the mixture. Leave the mixture on one side until cold.

Lightly grease a large baking tray. To make the pastry, melt the butter and then leave it to cool. Whisk together the olive oil and egg, stir in the yogurt, then, using a wooden spoon, stir the melted butter into the yogurt mixture, a little at a time, until smoothly mixed. Sift the flour, baking soda and salt together. Gradually stir the flour into the yogurt mixture to form a soft dough. Turn out on to a lightly floured surface and knead gently for a few minutes. Then roll the dough out to about ¼-inch thick. Using the rim of a glass about four inches in diameter, cut out circles from the pastry. Spoon

about two teaspoons of the filling on to one side of each circle. Fold the pastry over to form a semi-circular turnover. Press the edges to seal. Place on the baking tray and brush with a little egg yolk. Bake in a preheated oven, 400°, for about 20 minutes or until golden.
Serves 6

▲ *Aromatic vegetable turnovers with yogurt pastry*

AMBROSIAL APRICOT PRESERVES

This is even better flavored with elder-flowers instead of mint. Simply pull off the flowers and stir them into the apricot mixture. The elderflower version is the best preserves I have ever made.

4 pounds ripe apricots
1 cup freshly squeezed orange juice
4 tablespoons lemon juice
4 pounds sugar with pectin
1 tablespoon sweet butter
6 teaspoons chopped fresh mint or
   4–5 elderflower heads
3–5 tablespoons apricot brandy
   (optional)

Wash out six preserving jars and put them on a baking tray in a very low oven to sterilize them. Halve the apricots and remove but reserve the pits. Open about half or more of the pits with a nut cracker to take out the kernel. Boil the kernels in a saucepan of water for one minute, then drain.

Now put the kernels and apricot halves into a preserving pan. Place the orange juice in a measuring jug, add the lemon juice and bring the total liquid quantity up to 1½ cups with water. Add this liquid to the apricots. Put the preserving pan over the heat, bring to the boil and simmer the liquid for 10–15 minutes, or until the apricots are soft but not mushy.

Remove the pan from the heat and add the sugar, stirring until it dissolves. Then stir in the butter. Next, stir in the chopped mint. Return the pan to the heat, bring the preserves to the boil and boil rapidly for 4–5 minutes. If you have a sugar thermometer, it will tell you when setting point is reached; otherwise, put a drop of preserves on a cold saucer and place it in the freezing compartment of the refrigerator for one minute to see if it sets – you don't want the preserves to be too set. Remove any scum from the top of the mixture with a spoon. Add the apricot brandy, if using, and leave the preserves for 15 minutes before potting. Then remove the tray of warm jars from the oven and carefully ladle the preserves into them. Cover the tops of the jars with wax discs before sealing. Leave to cool.
Makes about 6 x 1 pound jars

EGGPLANT, APRICOT AND TOMATO CHUTNEY

4 ounces dried apricots, chopped
1½ cups freshly squeezed orange
   juice
2 eggplants
8 garlic cloves, very finely chopped
3-inch piece fresh root ginger, finely
   chopped
8 cardamom pods, roughly crushed
2 teaspoons cumin seeds
1 cup cider vinegar
3 tablespoons sherry vinegar
3 cups light brown sugar
2 x 13-ounce cans chopped
   tomatoes
2 teaspoons salt
½ teaspoon chili powder

Wash out four 1-pound preserving jars and place them on a baking tray in a very low oven to sterilize them.

Put the apricots into a bowl with the orange juice. Leave the apricots to soak for about one hour. Bring a saucepan of water to the boil, then cut the eggplants into 1-inch cubes and drop the cubes into the boiling water. Boil them for five minutes and then drain.

Put the soaked apricots and their juice, the eggplant, garlic and ginger, cardamom pods and cumin seeds into a large, heavy saucepan. Pour in both vinegars and stir in the sugar and the tomatoes. Add two teaspoons of salt.

Bring the mixture to the boil, then lower the heat and simmer gently in the open pan for 1½ to 1¾ hours, stirring occasionally at first and more often as the mixture thickens. Finally, season to taste with chili powder and more salt if necessary. Then spoon the chutney immediately into the sterilized jars. Seal the jars at once with plastic or vacuum covers.
TO SERVE This chutney is mild, but has an aromatic, sweet and sour taste. It is very good served with bread and cheese, with spicy dishes and with scrambled eggs.
Makes about 4 pounds

SWEET PICKLED SHALLOTS

1 pound shallots, peeled
4 tablespoons wine vinegar
1 cup extra virgin olive oil
   (approximately)
1 tablespoon clear honey
2 dried red chilies (optional)
Sea salt and black pepper

◀ *Ambrosial apricot preserves; eggplant, apricot and tomato chutney; sweet pickled shallots*

Put the whole shallots into a small saucepan with the vinegar and enough water to cover. Bring to the boil, then cover the pan and simmer gently for 30–45 minutes or until the shallots are soft right through. Then drain them and toss them in the oil. Place the shallots on a baking tray and put them under a fairly hot broiler for a few minutes, turning them once or twice, until they are dark brown to black in patches. Put them into a bowl with the honey and a sprinkling of sea salt and pepper. Mix together gently. Pack the shallots into one or two jars, cover them completely with olive oil, and leave to cool. Add a couple of chilies to each jar, if using. Then put on well-fitting covers and store in a cool, dark place.
TO SERVE You can use these as an hors d'œuvre or appetizer, with good bread to soak up the oil.

MENUS

The sequence and balance of a meal is as important as the taste of the food itself, and as much care should go into thinking about the character and impact of the dishes in relation to each other as the culinary skill required to prepare them. It is not only the stomachs but also the emotions of your guests you have to think of.

The first course should titillate and excite, the main course satisfy and intrigue, and the dessert induce, at its best, sheer ecstasy. Although you may want to concentrate on one national cuisine or theme – you may want to produce an Indian buffet for a party or a typically Italian family dinner, for example – the individual dishes should contrast with and complement each other, not just in their taste, but by considering texture, color, shape and even temperature. It may seem obvious, for instance, that you would not choose to sit down and eat three creamy, pale-colored dishes one after another, but it is surprising how often just this sort of menu is offered simply through lack of forethought.

It can be particularly difficult to get a mix of tastes and textures in a completely vegetarian dinner party or family lunch menu. A mixture of different but complementary vegetable dishes can be successful,

but a focal centerpiece of some kind always gives more shape to the occasion. If you choose something like a vegetable pie, make sure that your preparation of the accompanying vegetables and vegetable dishes don't clash with it. You wouldn't want to serve a carrot and corn pie, accompanied by more root or starchy vegetables, for example. Even more than with a meal containing meat or fish, vegetable dishes must be of different character and color.

When you are putting together a menu, it is also important to judge people's appetites. The first course must never be enough actually to satisfy hunger; in fact, it should remind people of the pleasure of eating and make them look forward even more to the rest of the meal. The main course should, by contrast, never leave you still feeling hungry, but you should not feel bloated either. If you are just about full, room can somehow always be found for a tempting dessert – and if you have served a rich main course, the dessert should be light and refreshing. If the main course is light, you may wish to serve an extra course – a salad, perhaps, or cheese before the dessert.

On the following pages there are some suggestions for menus – vegetarian and non-vegetarian (or 'practically vegetarian') – for a variety of occasions.

BRUNCH

*Brunch is rather a nice idea for vacations when you want to get up late and have
one meal which combines two. It is a far more formal meal than breakfast and
guests are usually invited, but it can also be very relaxed.*

FOR NON-VEGETARIANS

Three-cheese custard *(38)*

Smoked fish and sesame balls with tomato sauce *(84)*

Baked sandwiched eggplant *(53)*

White pear cake *(139)*

FOR VEGETARIANS

Egg, cheese and onion gratin with cherry tomatoes *(43)*

Dried fava bean purée with green vegetables *(55)*

Braised red cabbage with chestnuts and peas *(50)*

Carrot tart with candied carrot topping *(139)*

CHILDREN'S LUNCH

*With fussy children, meals can be tricky. However, they always seem to like
cheesy dishes, pasta and chicken. Even children who are difficult about eating
vegetables seem to accept them when they are combined with these things.*

FOR NON-VEGETARIANS

Vietnamese chicken noodle hotpot
with fresh leaves *(95)*

Ken Buggy's Irish soda bread *(145)*

Fruit in passion fruit cream *(131)*

FOR VEGETARIANS

Leek and red onion cobbler
with potato and cheese pastry *(121)*
OR
Spaghetti with peas, scallions and pea, mint and sour
cream sauce *(32)*

Honey-glazed fresh apricot tart *(135)*

PICNIC

*Picnic food must be portable. However, some dishes can be carried in the pan
or dish they were made in, and kept warm, which always seems a special treat on
a cold day. Above all, you must avoid sandwiches!*

FOR NON-VEGETARIANS

Exotic chicken pie *(105)*

Anchovy, garlic and parsley sticks *(148)*

Greek salad bread *(147)*

Squidgy prune, pecan, citrus
and honey cake *(143)*

FOR VEGETARIANS

Lentil tart with rice crunch pastry *(34)*

Devonian Spanish omelet *(43)*

Tomato, herb, Parmesan and garlic bread with
olive oil *(151)*

Citrus-drenched cake *(143)*

Sunday lunch

A Sunday morning spent listening to music and cooking for my family and friends is one of my favorite times. Sunday lunch is an informal, relaxed affair; it needs no first course, but to me a proper dessert is essential.

FOR NON-VEGETARIANS

Roast chicken with zucchini and cranberry sauce *(105)*

Tuscan fava beans *(53)*

Goddess of Puddings *(141)*

FOR VEGETARIANS

Garden pie *(121)*

Sautéed leeks with pumpkin seeds and steamed snow peas *(57)*

Sharp lemon soufflé on a chocolate shortbread base *(137)*

Summer lunch

When weather and location permit, it is pleasant to eat outdoors. Even if you can't, the food should make the most of seasonal ingredients. You can have several smaller dishes for a vegetarian meal instead of a heavier main course.

FOR NON-VEGETARIANS

New potatoes with quails' eggs and herby cream cheese mayonnaise *(15)*

Stuffed salmon with Mediterranean sauce *(75)*

Peach, arugula and mixed leaf salad with rose petals and rose water dressing *(59)*

Honey-glazed fresh apricot tart *(135)*

FOR VEGETARIANS

Chilled zucchini, avocado and yogurt soup *(21)*

Fresh plum tomato and basil tart with olive oil and garlic crust *(9)*

Anglo-Syrian bread *(147)*

Green salad with spring flowers *(65)*

Rose petal sherbet with crystalized petals *(141)*

Family dinner

Cozy and informal, this is almost my favorite kind of meal. It is a chance to make delicious dishes which need eating immediately and are impractical for formal meals or larger gatherings – and you can forget about a first course, too.

FOR NON-VEGETARIANS

Chicken and spinach pasta pie *(31)*

Endive, avocado, cherry tomato and walnut salad *(68)*

Upside-down apple tart with orange and oatmeal pastry *(126)*

FOR VEGETARIANS

Cauliflower cheese with sun-dried tomatoes, fresh red chili and crunchy Parmesan topping *(37)*

Sautéed leeks with pumpkin seeds and steamed snow peas *(57)*

White pear cake *(139)*

FORMAL DINNER PARTY

A formal dinner party can be very enjoyable to prepare. But in order to feel relaxed, shop the day before, and make the first course or the dessert well in advance too. The dishes should have a minimum of last-minute cooking.

FOR NON-VEGETARIANS

Pink trout balls with dill vinaigrette *(16)*

Pumpkin stuffed with spiced turkey and cashew nuts *(93)*

Chinese salad with bean sprouts and crispy spiced garlic *(67)*

Ricotta and dark chocolate ice cream cake *(125)*

FOR VEGETARIANS

Avocados in spinach jelly with garlic and chilli *(15)*

Leek and eggplant charlotte with sun-dried tomatoes *(109)*

Sautéed mushrooms and broccoli with garlic and coriander seeds *(49)*

Raspberry and orange parfait in a chocolate case *(129)*

SUMMER BUFFET PARTY

Buffet parties usually offer too many different dishes. Since people often put a little of everything on their plates, it is vital to plan dishes which enhance each other. Prepare the food in advance and either eat cold or reheated.

FOR NON-VEGETARIANS

Shrimp and smoked haddock mousse with scallop sauce *(12)*

Endive, avocado, cherry tomato and walnut salad *(68)*

Steamed chicken balls with coriander leaf mayonnaise *(99)*

Green salad with spring flowers *(65)*

Apricot, rosemary and honey soufflé *(126)*

A bowl of raspberries or strawberries and a bowl of crème fraîche

FOR VEGETARIANS

Exotic egg and cucumber salad with coconut and yogurt sauce *(67)*

Shallot and scallion tart with crunchy hot butter pastry *(11)*

Wild rice salad with cucumber and fresh orange *(71)*

Garbanzo bean, feta cheese and tomato salad with green chili and lemon dressing *(73)*

Chocolate cake with vanilla and cinnamon *(143)*

A bowl of raspberries or strawberries and a bowl of crème fraîche

INDEX

THE AUTHOR

Josceline Dimbleby is one of Britain's most popular and most innovative food writers. Her books have sold more than two million copies worldwide. She is food correspondent of the *Sunday Telegraph* and contributes regularly to other newspapers and magazines. She is particularly noted for the inventiveness and originality of her recipes which often feature brilliantly successful and unexpected combinations of ingredients. Josceline spent much of her childhood abroad, especially in the Middle East and in South America and she has traveled extensively in India and the Far East. Her unceasing flow of ideas for recipes comes in part from her familiarity with a wide range of international cuisines.

Editorial Director Sandy Carr
Recipes Editor Pam Cary
Assistant Editor Anne Cochrane
Art Director Jason Vrakas
Art Editor Sara Kidd
Design Assistant Adelle Morris
Photographer Simon Wheeler
Home Economist Allyson Birch
Assistants to Allyson Birch Teresa Goldfinch,
Jane Stevenson
Stylist Rebecca Gillies
Indexer Naomi Good
Production Charles James

The author and publishers would like to thank the following people who helped to test the recipes:

Anne Bailey, Matthew Barrell, Lorna Bateson, Andrew Christodolo,
Penny and Luke Cunliffe, Gemma Hancock, Sara Harper, Fiona Holman,
Paul Jackson, Charles and Saskia James, Rosanna Merrell, Suzanne Morris,
Lyn Parry, Margaret Rand, Clifford Rosen, John Worsfold